Hathersage
IN THE PEAK

*

A History

Hathersage and the High Peak

HATHERSAGE
IN THE PEAK

✳

A History

BARBARA A. BUXTON

Phillimore

2005

Published by
PHILLIMORE & CO. LTD
Shopwyke Manor Barn, Chichester, West Sussex, England

ISBN 1 86077 348 6

Printed and bound in Great Britain by
MPG BOOKS LTD
Bodmin, Cornwall

Contents

List of Illustrations

Acknowledgements

I wish to thank the staff in the John Rylands Library, Manchester, Lichfield Joint Record Office, Derbyshire County Record Office and Local Studies Library, and Sheffield Archives and Local Studies Library for their invaluable help.

I am indebted to His Grace, the Duke of Devonshire and the Chatsworth Settlement Trustees for allowing me to read in Chatsworth House library and for permission to reproduce the 1618 tithe list. I am beholden to Michael Shuttleworth Esq. for allowing me access to his family's papers. The Warden of Launde Abbey gave much appreciated help on my visit.

I thank Susanne Mitchell who read the manuscript in the early stages and encouraged and Anne Slater for giving me the chance to read her unpublished thesis of 1991. The Rev. J. Allum and Rev. D. Pickering helped by making the Hathersage parish registers available.

Many people have made a contribution in giving me information especially J. Addison, D. Baker, M. Burkinshaw, A. Chatburn, J. Cox, J. Flood, J. Furness, N. Fletcher, J. Froggatt, G. Platts, M. and K. Rotherham, B. Smith, M. Sunderland, A. and B. Ward. I am obliged to all of them.

I am grateful to those who have lent photographs, P. Bowyer, J. Cottam, J. Cox, J. Hardwick, S. Humphreys, J. Marsden, D. Mellor, D. Moseley, M. Newton, M. Prigent, H. Rodgers, M. Shuttleworth, A. Simpson, J. Stone, K. and A. Wilson, B. Wilson, C. Wragg. Every effort has been made to trace copyright holders and I apologise for any unintentional omission.

I am indebted to the following for permission to reproduce illustrations or maps: Dean and Canons of Christ Church, Oxford (Lady Montacute's tomb no. 27); Derbyshire Archaeological Society (1791 Burdett Map of Derbyshire no. 46); Derbyshire County Council Cultural and Community Services (North Lees Hall no. 38); Derbyshire County Council and Buxton Museum & Art Gallery (Roman artefacts, nos. 10, 11, 12); National Trust, Hardwick Hall (The Devonshire Collection); (6th Earl of Shrewsbury no. 36); National Gas Archives N.G.T. (two gasholders no. 95); Redditch Borough Council, Forge Needle Mill Museum (Needle scourer's bench no. 72); Severn Trent Water (Birchinlee, Howden and Ladybower Dams, nos. 90, 92, 118); Sheffield Art Galleries and Museum Trust (Roman head no. 9); Sheffield City Council, Head of Leisure Activity Services (Sketch of 18th-century Hathersage in panoramic landscape no. 49).

Special thanks are due to David Hart without whose skills and interest this book would not have seen the light of day. My family have revealed previously undiscovered talents and expertise and their help was much appreciated.

To Keith my deepest thanks for his patience and support.

Introduction

Hathersage today is a village in the Hope Valley surrounded by hills on the edge of the Peak District and eight miles from Sheffield. It has a population of about two thousand people and a steady stream of tourists. It lies on the lower slopes of the dramatic hillsides under the high rock Edges. It has two churches, a chapel and nonconformist groups. There are two banks, a post office, fire station, leisure facilities including a swimming pool and a library bus that comes once a week. There are shops, pubs and places to eat and it has a railway link with Manchester and Sheffield.

The early village stood near its church on the hill above the flood plains of the River Derwent, its houses close to the brooks, springs and wells that today are celebrated in Derbyshire by an annual well dressing of flowers. Where three farmhouses and an inn once stood alone among fields on the main street, buildings have sprung up since the early 19th century. The orientation of roads has changed and the great curve of the main road up the hill was once a junction of two turnpike termini at Hathersage Hall and its width at Dog Kennel has swallowed the little island of buildings that once stood there. Where the Smithy Meadow estate now stands at the edge of the curve, there was, even in the early 20th century, pasture edged with trees.

Although the village is small, the far-flung boundaries of the manor and parish of Hathersage are recorded in the occasional Perambulations of the past when respected men of the village walked the boundaries to check and remember the defining landmarks

1 *Hathersage in its setting in the High Peak.*

2 *Church Bank in 1906.*

for the next generation. The walk began at Abbey Side high above the modern dams to the north, moving towards the south-east to the next manors, down to the River Derwent and back northward again to Abbey Side. We will become familiar with these places but not the village of Derwent, once in the parish, for it was inundated to make Ladybower Reservoir in 1943.

Very often village issues creep over its boundaries and we have sometimes to look beyond them to complete the story. Sometimes they are the cause of legal disputes between parishes: families straddle the borders, estates stretch into a field across the river or hill ridge defining the limit of parish and manor. People crossed the Yorkshire divide to find a gentler valley in which to farm and marry.

The legendary Little John of Robin Hood fame may have lived here and some say he lies in the churchyard. Charlotte Brontë once visited and used the familiar Eyre surname for her heroine in *Jane Eyre*. Too much is made of the status of the medieval Eyres of Padley and not enough of their achievements as men of business and stewards of great landowners. The Elizabethan North Lees House we see today was an Eyre home only for a generation or two, when they were tenants, but later Eyres of Highlow Hall across the River Derwent and over the parish boundary became a dynasty of some consequence.

The story begins with the archaeology of the surrounding moors, once forested and now covered with summer scented heather. To the west, Neolithic life flourished on Offerton and Eyam Moors. To the east, on the highland below Stanage Edge and overlooked by Higger Tor and Carl Wark, Early Bronze-Age communities became less nomadic, beginning to farm the lower slopes and developing their tools and implements to work the heavier soils.

In the Middle Ages the outskirts of the manor were the hunting grounds of manorial lords and the grazing lands of monastic grange farms, established by distant mother

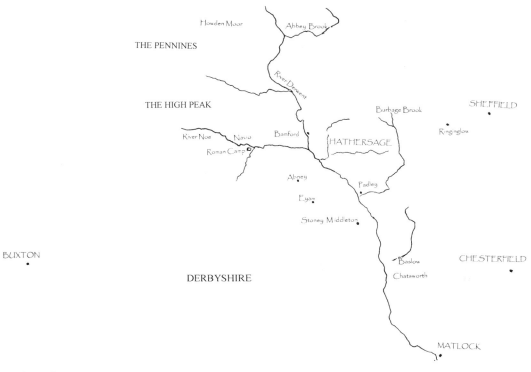

3 *Hathersage in the Peak.*

4 *River Derwent at Leadmill.*

houses. We meet medieval lords of the manor, church builders and bandits. There will be tales of lawlessness in Edward II's reign and of people summoned to Agincourt and the defence of England against the Armada.

Here the Fitzherberts of Norbury acquired Padley Hall, and in the 1530s reunited the divided lordship of Hathersage for the first time in centuries. Adhering to the old religion, they fell foul of the Elizabethan religious settlement. Thomas died in the Tower of London in 1591, and his brother living at Padley also died in prison. National events have moulded Hathersage whether in the turmoil of Stuart England or the gradual changes of the Industrial Revolution. In the last century its men and women went to war and Blitz victims found a home here. Its Millennium celebrations are now part of its history, too.

The purpose of this book is to show the role of Hathersage in a changing nation, its history still to be found in records and rare sources. It is dedicated to those who inspired this search and wanted to know more.

Lords of the Manor of Hathersage

Chief Lords

These had many other 'honours' and manors.

Pre-1066 Leofnoth and Leofric, Anglo-Saxon thanes, held jointly, with Crich manor
By 1087 Ralph Fitz Hubert, Baron Crich
   1135 Richard Basset
  1200s Sir Ralph Frecheville, Baron Crich
  1300s de Bellers, Baron Crich
  1500s Earl of Shrewsbury, Baron Crich
  1600s Shrewsbury line died out in Civil War period

Lesser Lords

  1263 Matthew de Hathersage died. Lordship divided between descendants

1264 *Longford heirs*	*Gousill heirs*
	Sell share of manor to Thorps in 1400s
1537 Sir William Holles buys	
1551 Sir Thomas Fitzherbert buys	1555 Sir Thomas Fitzherbert buys too

Hathersage manor now under one lord, Sir Thomas Fitzherbert, by 1555
  1591 Thomas Fitzherbert Esq., who died 1614
  1592 Estate disputed, long legal cases
  1657 Fitzherberts sold lordship to
      Rowland Morewood Esquire of Norton near Sheffield
      Edward Pegge Esquire of Beauchief near Sheffield
      Humphrey Pegge of Ashbourne
      They were related distantly to the Eyres by marriage. Descendants sold
        to descendants of Bess of Hardwick
  1705 Duke of Newcastle of Worksop who sold to cousin in 1743
  1743 Duke of Devonshire, his successor dukes are lord to present day

Chapter 1

Beginnings

History begins when men can tell us in some way how they lived, worshipped and committed their dead. Hathersage is empty of prehistoric clues, a nameless hillside with water pouring down the slopes into a wide flood plain of the River Derwent, a terrain where men of the Early Stone Age could not live. But the moorsides and summits overlooking the modern village were to become rich in signs of Neolithic and Early Bronze-Age settlement.

It is something of a miracle that any evidence remains on the high moor surrounding Hathersage after six thousand years, bearing in mind the unscientific methods and impatient spades of archaeologists of the 18th and 19th centuries and the proximity of a large urban population in Sheffield. The area of north Derbyshire is archaeologically important. Recently Early Stone-Age cave art dated *c.*10000 B.C. has been found at Cresswell Crags, some twenty-five miles to the east, where other signs of Early Stone-Age human habitation exist. At Earl Sterndale near Buxton and other nearby sites there have been finds of arrowheads and flint tools. In this period, people were nomadic hunters who made summer migrations to follow their prey on the limestone uplands of the White

5 *Higger Tor overlooking Carl Wark where a stone wall indicates a possible Neolithic or Bronze-Age defensive site.*

Peak. They could make fire but not
build.

By 4000-3000 B.C. farming
in the White Peak was beginning.
Although the hunter-farmers made
seasonal hunting tours, they were
becoming less mobile. Evidence
shows that in this period tamed
animals were herded into closed
pasture and hardy cereals grown
in small enclosures with primitive
walling. No authenticated dwellings
have been found but it is safe to
presume that they were thatched
pit huts.

6 *Bronze-Age cairn with Higger Tor in the background.*

The Neolithic Age brought
new life into the Peak, which was always marginal for agricultural use. By 2500-1800
B.C. the climate had improved by two or three degrees centigrade and the population was
increasing. The need for more food encouraged people to farm and hunt on the uplands
at heights of 1,000 to 1,500 feet where the thin soil could be worked by Neolithic
tools that were no match for wetter, heavier soils elsewhere. Later colonies moved to
the gritstone heights of Stanage, Bamford and Toothill in the Hathersage region.

While Stonehenge was in its final enlargement, stone circles began to appear in the
Peak. Arbor Low near Monyash was the first ritualistic centre in the area and examples
have also been found on Offerton Moor and Wet Withins near Eyam. Local communities
made these sacred ceremonial circles for public occasions when agreements were sworn
and treaties and laws proclaimed by the leaders. These circles, with associated cairns
and field systems, are no less than 3,600 years old and appeared over a period of 2,000
years.

Men did not have the tools to dig graves for their dead. Interment in caves was
common and rock fissures were used to expose bodies to the elements. Some artefacts
relating to these committals have been found near Hathersage at Abney, Eyam and
Castleton. When important people died, they were buried in chambered tombs, barrows
and cairns, which occur locally.

On the western slopes of the Hope Valley, near Highlow and Offerton, Early Bronze-
Age sites were opened in the 18th and 19th centuries but were damaged or disturbed
by the excavators. In some cases few traces remain because artefacts and stone tools were
removed without mapping. Not all early archaeologists were irresponsible. Thomas Bateman
of Lombdale Hall near Youlgrave made a study of sites in Derbyshire over the years from
1843 to 1861 and recorded and drew what he found. By modern standards he worked
too quickly but he is a worthy forerunner of today's archaeologists, whose painstaking
research and techniques ensure that sites are preserved and better understood.

To the north-east of Hathersage the colonists of the Early Bronze Age have left
numerous traces, saved partly because of the neglect of these earlier researchers, on the
moorland at Bamford Moor at about 1,000 feet, at Dennis Knoll, Sheepwash Bank,
Toothill, and close to Winyard's Nick and Toad's Mouth where there are many burial
and clearance cairns. The burial cairns are heaps of stones artificially assembled to cover
a body or bodies and protect them from desecration. Some cairns are oval but more are
circular; some have low terraced walls, now in a bad state but still visible in places. The
diameters tend to be 10 to 15 feet but can be larger. The height varies but some are

less than three feet now. It is remarkable that these cairns, some 3,000 to 4,000 years old, have survived the attentions of enclosure wall and turnpike road builders, sheep and modern walkers. These cairn fields or areas often have associated field systems. Chemical analysis of pollen found in soil deposits both at Royston and Big Moor suggests that there was mixed farming of pasture and hardy cereals at this period and it seems likely that the Early Bronze-Age communities of Bamford Moor, Stanage and Burbage farmed in the same way. Although these field systems and settlements are to be found between 1,000 and 1,500 feet the best situation was below 1,150 feet, while land over 1,300 feet inhibited settlement. Consequently Stanage Edge and Burbage Edge were too high to encourage settlement. So many cairns were made between Toad's Mouth and Winyard's Nick that there must have been a sizeable local community unless people travelled some way to burial centres, as is the case at Stanton Moor. The remains of stone huts on the edge of Lawrence Field close to Padley Gorge have sometimes been mistaken for Bronze-Age dwellings but they are medieval in origin, as are those in Sheffield Plantation across the Gorge.

During this long period advances were made by the Longhead and Beaker peoples. Their polished flint tools and clay drinking vessels originate elsewhere but have been found locally so it is clear that quite distant travel was possible. Bronze artefacts found in the Peak and Hope Valley were made and brought from as far away as Cumbria and Wales. In the Early Bronze Age the Beaker People buried their dead in a foetal position surrounded by tools and the collared and bell beakers from which they derive their name. As their skill developed in throwing clay to make beakers and later food vessels, it is possible to discern a sequence of human activity and a comparative chronology. Beaker-style food vessels have been found in cairns in neighbouring areas at Ashford in the Water, Baslow, Edensor, Longstone and Dronfield. As the practice of cremation developed, the collared urns of the period became the only evidence available to researchers. Cremation urns have been found at Totley, Crookes, Dronfield and Stanton Moor. Many later finds of the Mid-Bronze Age (1800-1000 B.C.) have been made nearer Hathersage, above Eyam and Baslow and Holmesfield, and isolated ones at Castleton, Foolow, Hazlebadge, Highlow, Hope and Outseats.

The Late Bronze-Age tribes, with more skills and finer tools, began to settle in lower areas with heavier soil at 800-1,000 feet where they could use the coppiced fringes of woodland for fencing and building their huts. Finds of cremation urns of this period

7 *A clearance cairn and a Neolithic Bronze-Age dwelling are excavated on Gardom Edge.*

8 *A Roman causeway near Stanage Pole on the moors to the east of Hathersage.*

have been made at Abney, Eyam Moor, Highlow and further afield, at Baslow, Bubnell and Big Moor.

Bronze-Age finds around Hathersage, at Outseats, Highlow, Leam Moor and Abney Grange, are only known to us from Pegge commenting in the 18th century on small lows with 'rude urns and burnt bones', but similar urn-finds near Sheffield give us some idea of man's artistic skill at this time; late in the period, ornamental beads of jet and amber were made.

And then this surge of human activity in the Peak began to decline. Something happened over a period of four hundred years from 1000 to 600 B.C. to deter people. There was certainly a deterioration of climate and the Peak District, always marginal land to cultivate, became yet more inhospitable. Even the long-lasting occupation of Roystone Grange near Ashbourne, and perhaps on Big Moor, ceased. The last local pottery found had become crude and ill-made. Sometimes a new 'Dark Age' arrives, when men forget their skills, and the Peak and north-east Derbyshire were no exception at this time. The Bronze Age here had been a progressive culture: people traded over the length and breadth of Britain and left memorials of their art; now it was all over. We do not know the reason for the end of this fertile period, whether a colder climate, conquest, plague or bad harvests.

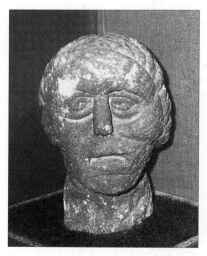

9 *The Romano-British head found in Hathersage (Sheffield City Museums Trust).*

The local population was to burgeon once more in the Iron Age when the hill forts of Mam Tor and possibly Carl Wark were made. Parts of a chain, the hill forts of Hope Valley define a warlike border between tense tribes continually under challenge. To the south were the Coriatani, one of the Iceni tribes living in the Midlands, and further to the north were the Brigantes, the dominant people of Northumbria and the Pennines. The earthwork hill forts may pre-date the Roman-named tribes but they almost certainly played their part as shelters in tribal attacks. They also tell of pressure of population on insufficient land and a desire for ore-bearing territory. By this time no one chose to live on inhospitable summits above the ubiquitous forests, where water was scarce. These forts were, more likely, occasional refuges in times of danger. In the case of Mam Tor,

10 *Dedication stone found at the Roman fort of Navio.*

the earthworks encircling an earlier encampment of *c.*12000 B.C. revealed few finds apart from store pots in what was a defensive site.

There are numerous theories about the Iron Age and the influx of Celtic culture. Some writers see an increasing occupation by the Brythonic Celts somewhere between 500 B.C. and A.D. 100. Others are less sure but see a common Belgic culture and a Celtic language moving across Britain, although there is very little evidence of their presence in the Hope Valley, where barrows and cairns were no longer made. There are no certain Iron-Age burials so far found in a wide area surrounding Hathersage.

The Romans were also to see the Hope Valley as part of a defensive line after they penetrated the more resistant north. Four miles to the west of Hathersage the first Roman fort of Navio at Brough was built *c.*A.D. 73, thirty years after the Roman invasion and during the governorship of Agricola, whose armies were to reach as far north as the Forth to Clyde line. It became part of a line of forts in the region, including one at Templeborough, east of Sheffield, and an earlier fort at Chesterfield dating back to Nero. To the north-west of Navio was Zertodalia (its Melandra name dates from the work of an 18th-century scholar), guarding the West Pennine route near Glossop. Navio fort at Brough supervised the important local lead-mining industry and kept watch on the Brigantian tribes who erupted into attack at times along the southern edge of the Pennines. The fort was sited on open rising ground at the confluence of Bradwell Brook and the River Noe.

Very few finds have been made at Navio or in the area. There is a dedication stone, possibly celebrating the new fort of Navio, giving details of the officers in charge and their cohort: 'In honour of [Emperor] Titus Aelius Antoninus Pius, erected by the First Cohort of the Aquitani under Julius Verus and the supervision of Capitonus Fuscus, Praefect of the Cohort.' The stone can be dated to the Emperor's reign of A.D. 138-61. An altar set up by another Praefect of the First Cohort of Aquitani at Navio can be seen at Haddon Hall. By the end of Navio's first phase, the army of Antoninus Pius was far to the north, consolidating a Forth-Clyde frontier with a turf wall named after him. It seems that, like some Pennine forts, Navio was evacuated sometime in the A.D 140s to supply troops for the Antonine Wall during a period of peace in the Peak.

The fort lay ungarrisoned for some years until the Brigantes again revolted against Roman rule. Originally a simple structure with an earthwork, ditch and timber buildings, Navio was reoccupied in A.D. 158 and modified in line with the standard fort design used throughout the Roman Empire, and it remained in continuous occupation for just on two hundred years. Its granary, an important store,

11 *Stone basin found at Navio fort.*

12 *Stone artefacts found in a strongroom at Navio fort and Hope (not the large altar).*

expected to hold enough grain to last at least two years, has been found. Outside the fort, to the south-east, signs of a possible trading settlement (vicus) of this period have been found.

From the middle of the second century A.D. for fifty years the First Cohort of Aquitanians formed the garrison at Navio. We also know that the Praefect Proculus commanded this garrison for a time and dedicated an altar stone to the god Hercules. The infantry unit of 500 Gallic auxiliaries was Romanised, although speaking a French patois as well as colloquial army Latin. The garrison supervised the local lead working using slaves from the local people to work the shallow mines. Not only lead was extracted, but also silver from the lead. Ingots found at Navio bear the official Latin authorisation of production and indicate whether silver had been extracted from the lead.

The garrison at Navio sought to live peacefully alongside the Britaniculi or 'little Britons'. The military regime did not encourage local deities and the way for inhabitants to get on was to adopt some form of Roman worship. This may explain the sculpted heads of goddesses found at Bradfield and Castleton. The finest head to be found locally so far is at Ecclesfield and the Hathersage example, by contrast, is crudely made.

Roman roads were built to link forts and towns and a fragment of the Zertodalia to Navio road has been found south of Hope's parish church. There is not yet certain identification of the route from Navio to Templeborough although there are traces of the original road on the moor toward Redmires near Sheffield.

The Aquitanians were not the only unit to garrison the Navio fort. Other Roman troops came and went from Navio, almost certainly including Saxon federates, the unpredictable allies often used by Rome in the late fourth century. The Navio garrison was finally withdrawn in A.D. 350 in the gradual and quiet decline of Roman control over sixty years which was almost complete by A.D. 400. By the early fifth century the garrison at Navio was long gone. We have no name for Hathersage in this period and probably only a few local families lived here, selling their cattle and corn to the legions. Fish and game and even prized hunting dogs may have found their way to the fort. Finds of Roman silver coinage cease in the A.D. 420s, and thereafter local ruling families emerged to control their own areas with varying degrees of efficiency. The Pax Romana in Britain had ended but its influence still lingered.

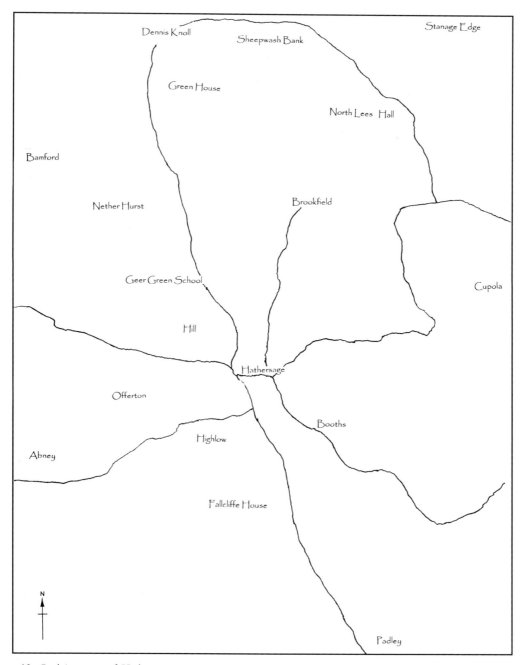

13 *Outlying areas of Hathersage.*

Chapter 2

Invasions

Hathersage featured little in the history of the Saxon invasions but the small community survived and eventually included a Danish military camp. The village had acquired a name by the time of the Normans. The coming of the Angles and Saxons, described by early writers such as Bede, was no sudden happening. Saxons had served much earlier as auxiliaries to the thinly stretched legions in Britain and elsewhere in the Roman Empire, and after A.D. 450 the Roman Emperor Marcian invited the Angles to defend Roman Britain against Irish and Pictish raiders. This would have had very little impact on the whole island but Angles and Saxons took home the word that the little island of Britain, with its inviting estuaries, was rich in pickings, much land unclaimed by existing British communities. Recurring plague in Europe in the A.D. 440s may have triggered a number of little invasions in the east of Britain and gradually the trickle became a flood of incomers.

Saxon settlement and beliefs pervaded the country and Roman Christianity was lost. St Germanicus was able to visit Britain twice before A.D. 440 but by A.D. 485 all ecclesiastical contact with the church in Europe was at an end. Churchmen resident in Britain lost heart and melted away or were not replaced when they died. An isolated religious community survived at Iona until the new Christian mission of A.D 596.

Britain had now become seven kingdoms that were often at war with each other about frontiers. Hathersage in the Peak, the area of the Pescatani tribes, so named by the Saxons, was on one such frontier on the line of the rivers Derwent and Don. It marked the northern limits of Mercia and the southern reaches of Northumbria, which, in spite of the glories of the Lindisfarne and Jarrow monastic culture and a golden age of peace, had fallen into decline. The southern Saxon kingdoms had accepted the overlordship of Wessex but the King of Northumbria remained independent until his famous submission in A.D. 829, without battle, at Dore, four miles from Hathersage. This sealed the authority of King Ecbert of Wessex over the Mercian area.

Saxon culture and Christianity were making an impact in the Peak. Stone crosses were focal places where inhabitants came to worship and listen to preachers in the open. The shaft of one such cross is to be seen in the present Hathersage churchyard and others are to be found at Bakewell, Eyam and Baslow. Saxon coffin lids have also been found in the area. Derbyshire lead was still worked and records show that some was sent from Wirksworth to Canterbury in A.D. 835. It is doubtful to which Saxon period local finds belong but they represent a distinctive culture developing over four hundred years, just as the Old English language of the Saxons was developing through four main regional dialects.

The earlier name of the present village of Hathersage was recorded as Hereseige in Domesday Book of 1086. The complexity of the languages of Old English and the Old Nordic of later Danes, with their regional changes over six hundred years, makes place-name translation a minefield of historical guesswork. A simple interpretation of

14 *A Saxon wayside cross in Hathersage churchyard.*

Hereseige may derive from *here* (invading army, Old English with 's' in the genitive form) and *ecg* (edge, OE). These are Old English words and therefore Saxon. In some parts of the Saxon Chronicles, *here* refers to the Danish army. We know from other sources that the area passed from Saxon to Danish occupation and then back again to Saxon control. It is likely, therefore, that local people or returning army leaders might call it 'Invaders' Edge'. We will never be entirely sure.

Local archaeology can help. Sometime in the Danish period, perhaps in the ninth century, the earthwork ramparts of Camp Green were erected above Hathersage, close to the site of the later medieval parish church. It is one of the largest known ringworks in north Derbyshire, being 80 feet in diameter and surrounded by a wide deep ditch. Controlling the pass eastward towards the plains of the River Don, its position suggests either a marker camp for an early push westward, or a defence post to monitor marauding Irish Vikings moving in from the north-west. Dr Richard Hodges of Sheffield University excavated a section and found at least two construction phases with a possible later use by the Normans.

The general settlement of Saxon England of A.D. 830 did not last long before the Norsemen of Scandinavia under Danish lordship came 'a-viking' or pirating. The first Viking raids to these shores are undateable but in A.D. 865 a large Danish army attacked Britain. It was a time of pillage, murder and treachery. Monasteries and churches were

15 *Part of the Danish earthworks of Camp Green fort.*

destroyed and monks and priests quailed before the new violence, leaving wayside crosses unvisited and their wooden churches closed. Some warriors penetrated the river estuaries and swept across the eastern and northern parts. By A.D. 874 they had annexed the Peak. We see the Danish presence in the local place-names on this north Mercian border, in Okerthorpe, Edensor, Winster, Derby and possibly Hope, while the Saxon neighbours identified Danish territory as Danesmoor, Danehill, Danes' Baulk and Dane Valley.

Further south, King Alfred of Wessex stopped the Danish advance into Wessex itself in A.D. 878. The Treaty of Wedmore, as well as imposing Christianity on the Danish leader, Guthrum, agreed the limits of Guthrum's territory. In the north the Danes began to settle and they established their customs, language and influence in areas including the Peak. Hathersage in its valleys and hills was to see both Saxon and Danish control and law and property were respected, but the peace did not survive. Wessex and the Danes competed for power north of the River Trent and a Danish army pushed southward beyond the Danelaw area in A.D. 892. The Mercian royal family, now joined to that of Wessex, ordered the building of the earthwork fort at Bakewell, only nine miles from Hathersage, to counter the Danish threat. The presence of the garrison was enough for Danish chiefs and the Scottish king, divided and fearful of each other, to make submission in A.D. 927 to the overlordship of Wessex.

However, anarchy and disruption broke out until the coming of Cnut, who became overall ruler of Scandinavia and England in the 10th century. The final invasion of William the Conqueror proved no transient foreign domination. By then Hathersage, a small community scratching a living on unrewarding soil above the flood plains of the Derwent, had a Saxon name derived from the passing influence of Danish armies.

Chapter 3

Domesday Book and Norman Hathersage

In 1086 there were ten families in the Hathersage area. We know this from the Inquest or, to give it its name a hundred years later, Domesday Book. This was a census of the taxable value of the whole of England although it was never completed in some areas. The two Domesday volumes of 1086 were meant to record the names and assets of the tenants-in-chief and the magnates who held 'honours' or estates. These were listed under counties although it was common for the owners' lands and manors to lie in more than one county. Hathersage was included in the honour of Ralph Fitz Hubert in Derbyshire but he had lands elsewhere, beyond the scope of this study. In answer to the questions required by royal commissioners or the overlord, it was recorded that

> In HERESEIGE Hathersage Leofnoth and Leofric had 2 carucates of land taxable. Land for 2 ploughs. Four outliers are attached to this manor, Bamford, Upper Hurst, half of Offerton and two parts of Stoney Middleton. In them, 2 carucates of land taxable. Land for 2 ploughs. Eight villagers, and 2 smallholders now have 5 ploughs. Wood and places of pasture 2 leagues long and 2 leagues wide. Value before 1066 60 shillings, now 30 shillings.

The entries were written in a clerk's Latin shorthand and represented tax values, not literal realities. Thus eight villagers and the two lowlier smallholder peasants would be the tax- or geld-paying heads of their household. The carucate was an earlier Danish measurement of land and the outliers were hamlets or, as some think, barleyfarms. 'Ploughs', for Domesday clerks, represented a recognised calculation of time, area and value. That two and two ploughs could become five has sometimes been interpreted as including assart, or new fields on uncultivated land.

The manor was a Norman concept new in England, the term gradually evolving to mean a hall and demesne or private seigneurial farm. Regulated by the lord's steward, reeve and the manorial court, the villagers, smallholders or slaves worked on the demesne two or three days a week, with extra boon service when needed, and on their own strips in designated open fields in the time left. Cereals and crops were grown in rotation each season with one field lying fallow. Animals grazed the common land, moor, wastes and sometimes woods under what later became strictly regulated conditions. Eventually the community became a village or 'town'. Unlike the neighbouring manor of Hope, with a much larger population, Hathersage in 1086 had no mill, church or priest.

Leofnoth and Leofric held the manor in 1066. These two thanes held other manors in Derbyshire including Crich, of importance later; such a double or even multiple holding was not uncommon in pre-Norman estates. There may have been other holders after them and before Ralph Fitz Hubert in 1085. It is important to realise that Hathersage was very close to royal estates. The King himself held the other half of the Offerton outlier in the manor of Hope and a third part of Stoney Middleton as part of his own land, while the other parts of these outliers belonged to the Hathersage manor. Other royal land nearby was held by William Peveril, possibly a natural son of William I, who built Peak (Peveril) Castle in addition to Bolsover Castle further east. Hathersage had woodland and pasture, a mix of open and forested terrain not unlike the New Forest today, which was calculated at two leagues square, which is about six miles long and six miles wide.

It is unlikely that the reduced value in 1086 of Hathersage, like so many other manors in the area, was due to the 'wasting of the North'. The wasting took place around York and to the north where William personally put down the Northern Rising in 1069. His campaign of destruction continued into 1070 but was cut short when he was obliged to make a forced march across the northern hills to Cheshire to stop risings there, and by 4 April he was in Salisbury for Easter.

The explanation of the reduced value of some Derbyshire manors, including Hathersage which halved in value, is controversial. The number of people in a village affected its value less than the attitude of the lord himself. Values were maintained on royal manors, and William Peveril's manors seemed to increase in value, but distant lords were less interested in their remote lands and may have taken over manors affected by changes after the Conquest. Two manors were sometimes merged and it is known that the accountant's solution was to write off the lost manor as 'waste' when families were moved elsewhere. Hathersage remained a small tax-paying community close to royal estates.

Chapter 4

The Medieval Lords of Hathersage

In the early Middle Ages the king owned all of England, granting tenancies in chief or 'honours' to bishops, priors, Norman leaders, Saxon earls and thanes. He remained a personal owner of vast territories run by castellans, sergeants and subtenants. Under the chief lord there could be lesser lords, and although protection was provided by the social fabric the peasants or villagers gradually lost their earlier Saxon freedoms and the duties and obligations to their immediate lord increased.

Fitz Hubert, Baron of Crich

Domesday Book records that the Fitz Huberts in or before 1086 held in Derbyshire alone 27 manors including that of Hathersage. Their chief holding in the area was the Barony of Crich. Hathersage was a manor subject to this barony and whoever held Crich barony in the future held Hathersage. The Fitz Hubert family name eventually became extinct due to lack of male heirs but a daughter, Julian, heir of Hubert, Baron Crich, married Sir Ralph Frecheville and the Barony of Crich survived.

Basset

Meanwhile another family became associated with Hathersage. By 1135 Richard Basset, Chief Justiciar to Henry I, together with his wife Maude, had built a small church in Hathersage as one of 17 designed to support and fund with tithes the Augustinian Canons' priory of Launde Abbey in Leicestershire, of which he was a co-founder. No records remain for the actual date of the building of Hathersage church but it was probably within ten years of the building of Launde Abbey *c.*1130. The Bassets were powerful at court and intermarried with the Furnivals of Sheffield. Although there is no reference to his status in the parish and manor, it seems likely that Richard held some level of lordship for a time.

The Meynils

Sixty years later another family, the Meynils, had an interest in the manor of Hathersage as lesser lords. They held land in the Scarsdale honour going back to 1085, including nearby Totley and Holmesfield as well as Eckington, Barlborough and Kinewaldermarch (Killamarsh) further to the east, which they held under the de Stuteville family or under the king himself.

The Meynils were a large family and each branch held separate estates. Our story starts with Robert de Meynil, who by 1195 had died leaving two young daughters. The two sisters, Annora and Alicia, were committed to the protection of the Crown and became wards of King Richard until a relation by marriage, Sewill Fitz Henry, bought the wardship for 50 marks from the Regent Prince John acting for King Richard in his absence.

Matthew de Hathersage – lesser lord

Being a guardian of heiresses was lucrative. Profit could be made from their wealth and their marriages and, in due course, Annora married Matthew de Hathersage, who enters the story for the first time, and Alicia Meynil married Adam de Gridling. Matthew de Hathersage held much land elsewhere in Derbyshire and Nottinghamshire. In the Barlborough area his overlord was de Stuteville. In Hathersage we know he held land valued in 1242 at 'half a knight's fee' under de Frecheville, Baron of Crich. A knight's fee was a form of tax assessment which was applied to landholders whether knights or not. A fraction of the fee was a very common form of assessment.

Three de Hathersage names appear in records, Hugo, Roger and Matthew. There is no evidence to show their relationship but it seems likely that a group of close kin held land locally, owing fealty and military service to the de Stutevilles or Baron Crich. In 1212 Hugo de Hathersage was excused from scutage tax 'for Wales', probably because he had served there. Roger de Hathersage appeared in a list of offenders in the Court of Forest Pleas. Matthew appeared in a document obtaining property in 1228. He was listed in contemporary subsidy and scutage tax lists and also appeared in other records. In 1251 (35 Henry III, Pipe Roll No. 95) he fell foul of the King over a forest encroachment and was fined 20 marks for encroaching on Buckstall Forest, probably a definition rather than a place. What is not clear is if he kept it as a park thereafter on payment of a fine, as was not uncommon. Matthew was also a patron of Welbeck Abbey, which had already been granted vast tracts of woodland above Hathersage on the hills west of the River Derwent by Prince John, as Earl of Mortain, in King Richard's reign. Matthew himself made grants to this Premonstratensian house to the south-east of the River Derwent, in the woodland within his own manor.

In 1258 Matthew and his wife Annora made a land grant regarding the church in Holme, at Dunston near Chesterfield, to the Prior of Lenton 'in return for a sparrow hawk'. Matthew was still paying feudal aids and scutage in 1259 but the Chancery Feet of Fines of 1263 makes it clear he had died by then.

On 22 September 1263 (47 Henry III), Annora, now a widow, was present at Lincoln at the official agreement of Chancery regarding an exchange of land between Matthew's heirs. Matilda de Gonshull (Goushill) and Nigel de Langeford (Longford) registered their agreement through their attorneys. Nigel de Longford was to release the Barlborough messuage, gardens and edifices then occupied by Annora in dower as widow of Matthew de Hathersage, and in return Matilda de Goushill would grant to Longford 'in perpetuity, the capital messuage with appurtenances in Hathersage which had belonged to Matthew de Hathersage'. All this was agreed in the presence of and with the consent of Annora, who was to keep the Barlborough messuage as dower only. Thus the Longfords gained control over the Hathersage land and lordship.

Matthew de Hathersage's death occurred during the baronial revolt led by Simon de Montfort, just before the King's victory at the Battle of Evesham in 1265. Matthew's name appears in a document after 1263 but it was not uncommon for a holder of land to be named even after his death in the slow transfer of legal realities. From then on the descendants were referred to as the 'heirs of Hathersage' in tax and other documents. In Edward I's reign, Agnes de Longford and Ada Gousill together had land in 'Haverseg', and still had it in 1302.

The Longfords

The Longford heirs to Matthew de Hathersage held lordship after 1263. The family was increasing in importance and in 1347 knighthood was bestowed on a later Nicholas

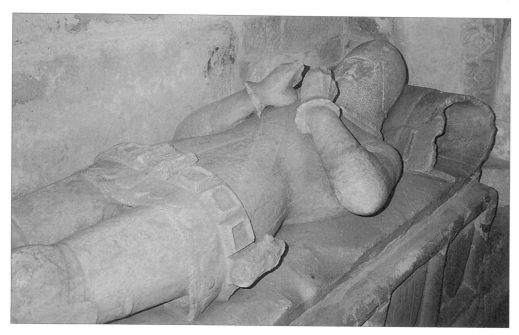

16 *Sir Nicholas Longford d.1357, a lord of Hathersage.*

Longford, for service at the English siege of Calais. The Inquisition Post Mortem of 1357, which records his estate at death, refers to Sir Nicholas Longford as sharing the town of Killamarsh with Thomas à Goushill but also holding half of the manor of Hathersage under the Frecheville overlords by service of an eighth part of a knight's fee. In other words, he shared lordship of Hathersage with the Gousils at that time.

In 1374 the Inquisition Post Mortem after the death of a later Sir Nicholas Longford stated that he held 'a moiety [half] of the site of the manor [of Hathersage], with five bovates of land, four acres of meadow, 60s. rent and a moiety of a watermill, held of Roger de Bellers, the Baron of Crich, by pledge of fealty only'. As tenant of the King in Killamarsh, he must supply a horse, a sack (a pike/hook) and a lance in the Welsh War. One hundred and thirty years later, another tenant in Hathersage, Robert Eyre, would hold land tenure in Hathersage under the Baron of Crich, by then the Earl of Shrewsbury. The Crich connection was still there. Chief lordship was never forgotten.

The Goushill name did not disappear from Hathersage after 1263 in spite of the agreement of that year. In 1330 a Robert de Newbold of Hathersage, chaplain, returned a 'moiety of the manor of Hathersage to Adam de Gousill and his wife Alice and their heirs forever to hold of themselves of the chief lord'. Although their main domiciles might be elsewhere, the Longfords farmed, hunted and lodged in Hathersage, and relations between the two families were not always smooth. In 1331 Adam Gousill was challenging Nicholas Longford in a court plea to claim his right to 'free warren' in Hathersage. Free warren was a licence from the king to lords of manors to hunt small game on their own estate.

By the early 15th century the Gousil portion had been acquired by the Thorps, their neighbours in their main area of influence on the borders of Nottinghamshire and Derbyshire. In a Feet of Fines of 1435, Stephen de Thorp junior and his wife paid 100 marks for 'a fourth part of the manor of Hathersage … to hold of themselves and

THE LONGFORD FAMILY

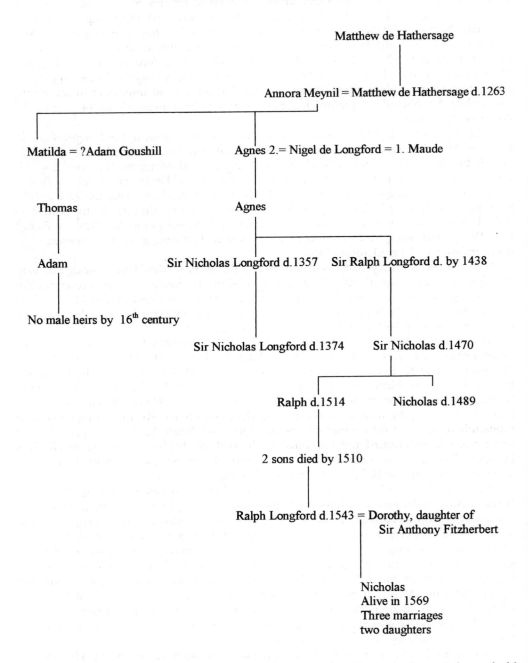

their heirs of her body of the Chief Lord forever'. The Thorps had no right to hold a court baron and it is clear that the Longfords and their trustees exercised the active and dominant role of local lordship. The Gousill connection with Hathersage was ended when the male line died out in Henry VIII's reign.

Meanwhile, the Sir Ralph Longford, listed in 1431 as holding a quarter knight's fee in Hathersage, had died by 1438. More is known of his son, Sir Nicholas Longford, who in 1460 granted for a time his manors of Longford and Hathersage to trustees including Nicholas Fitzherbert. At his death early in 1470 they returned the manors to the son and heir, the next Nicholas Longford. Soon power of attorney was restored to trustees including Nicholas Fiztherbert, who held the Longford manors of Longford, Newton Sulney and Hathersage until 1475. It is interesting to see the beginning of the connection between these three manors and the Fitzherberts, so important in the future. Meanwhile, Sir Nicholas Longford had been knighted by Edward IV in 1471 after the Battle of Tewkesbury.

The property arrangements were bound to lead to disharmony in the Longford family. By 1489 Sir Nicholas had died without issue. Sir Ralph, his younger brother, stood to inherit but the many complex holdings and the claims of Margaret, the widow of Sir Nicholas, led to a dispute settled eventually by the Earl of Derby. Sir Ralph Longford, supported by his long-term trustee, John Fitzherbert of Norbury, won the case against Margaret and inherited Hathersage with other estates in Lincolnshire, Nottinghamshire and elsewhere in Derbyshire. One of his leases as landlord grants 'to Thomas Wellys, John Wellys and Margery Bouynton of his manor of Hathersage to uses mentioned in other indentures 10th October 1496'.

The Longford family had been drawn into the Wars of the Roses through at least two generations. Many families had lost possessions by being on the wrong side at crucial stages of the wars, and it was with this experience in mind that in Henry VIII's second regnal year Sir Ralph made a will protecting his property by a deed of trust. In the event two sons had died before him by the year 1510.

It was a grandson, a new Ralph Longford, who inherited Hathersage and all the other Longford estates in 1514 (IPM 15 June, 5 Henry VIII). He married Dorothy Fitzherbert in 1522 and a son and heir was born in 1531. Thomas Fitzherbert, son and heir of Sir Antony Fitzherbert, Knight, was also Sir Ralph's brother-in-law and trustee. In the next year, however, Sir Ralph Longford sold to a Sir William Holles, one of his trustees elsewhere, the manors of Hathersage, Barlborough and Killamarsh together with thousands of acres of land, meadow, pasture, gorse and heath. Sir William paid £1,200 and Sir Ralph quitclaimed and warranted for himself and his heirs to renounce all claim in future. The sale was reaffirmed in 1537 when Holles bought yet more land in the three manors from Sir Ralph and his wife Dorothy.

Sir Ralph Longford's son was five years old, when Sir Ralph was selling the estates. It was a curious decision, but lords with many manors bought and sold them frequently. They might wish to consolidate in one area, or to accommodate new marriage alliances or to transfer property to other members of the family. Fear of the possible depredations of royal wardship might also influence them. The Dissolution of the Monasteries may have affected the timing of the Holles/Longford transaction. The sale was not the only legal paper in which Sir Ralph Longford and Dorothy, his wife, warranted for themselves 'against William, Abbot of St Peters, Westminster', better known now as Westminster Abbey. It is clear that the abbey had rights of patronage in their property and could have blocked the whole transaction but in 1537, in the monastic crisis, it would be powerless to challenge the transfer of land.

When Sir Ralph died in 1543, his son Nicholas, aged 12, inherited. He was still living in 1569, the year of the Herald's Visitation of Derbyshire. He had no sons but two daughters who made good marriages out of the area. Just as the Meynil sisters began the connection with Hathersage in 1195, so the Longford connection ended with two other sisters some three hundred years later.

Chapter 5

Nobles, Notables and Neighbours

By the 12th century the manor of Hathersage, once the honour of Fitz Hubert by 1086, had been granted to other lords, namely the de Bellers of Leicestershire and, by the late Middle Ages, the Earls of Shrewsbury. The title common to each successive lord was the Barony of Crich by which Hathersage was held. The Earl of Shrewsbury was descended from the Furnivals, the great family of Sheffield, who were only tenants at Bamford on Longford land in Hathersage as late as 1355, although their descendants would own more than a quarter of the land by 1504, as well as its lordship.

By the later Middle Ages, the neighbouring Royal Duchy of Lancaster included much of Derbyshire and the Peak District, with land and mineral interests in the Hope Valley and to the north-west. The Duchy influenced its close neighbour, the manor of Hathersage, for centuries. In the 1808 Hathersage Enclosure Act the Duke of Lancaster was named as one of the petitioners.

Other neighbouring aristocracy included the de Frechevilles, who still give their name to part of Sheffield. The Deincourt family of east Derbyshire and west Nottinghamshire were connected by marriage with the Thorps. The Thorp family held land at Thorpe near Newark in Edward II's reign and occasionally made land exchanges with the Gousills. In the 14th century Alice Deincourt married Sir Nicholas Longford (died 1356), and so the Thorps would have known of the Gousill inheritance in Hathersage. As we have seen, they acquired the Gousill portion of Hathersage in the 15th century.

The Fitzherberts played a part in Hathersage affairs by being trustees of the Longford lords. The policy of having trustee tenants was a wise precaution in the aftermath of the Wars of the Roses, especially as early deaths meant frequent changes in the Longford succession to the family estates. Two long minorities also put that family at a disadvantage and subject to the influence of trustees and tenants. One of their early tenants was Nicholas Fitzherbert and the Fitzherbert connection with Hathersage was to continue through three generations. The marriage between Thomas Fitzherbert and Anne Eyre in 1535 followed a policy

17 *Lord Harmon Belers (Bellers). The Bellers became chief lords of Hathersage.*

begun long before to acquire more property and standing in Hathersage. The climax of the family connection was when by 1555 Thomas Fitzherbert had bought both the lesser lordships.

Other influential families included the Padleys and Bernaks. The latter were a local family and a Bernak had once held the prestigious post of Bailiff of the Peak; they were also in Edward II's exclusive list of allies, the Corpus Comitatus of 1318. They had marriage ties with the Padleys of Padley Hall, who had numerous land holdings in Hathersage, and the Bernak device appeared on the Padley coat of arms. The Eyres of Padley were to use it as part of their own heraldic pretentions after the marriage in 1308 of Joanne de Padley to Robert Eyre. By virtue of his wife's inheritance in Hathersage and Padley, the family became the tenants and client gentry of the Earl of Shrewsbury, their chief lord.

The Plumpton family too had Hathersage connections. Although Yorkshire clients and stewards of the important Percy family, in the 15th century they married well and consequently acquired property in Derbyshire. By the 1480s Robert Eyre acted as local steward and close adviser to the Plumptons and the relationship was eventually sealed in 1500 with a marriage between Robert Eyre III's son, Arthur Eyre, and Margaret Plumpton. One of Margaret's ancestors was Alice Foljambe, of another illustrious family whose heraldic device included a leg in armour, obviously a pun on their name. It would find its way into the heraldic badge of the Eyres of Highlow in the 17th century.

Chapter 6

The Parish Church

Achurch for Hathersage was not listed in Domesday Book. There was a plain Saxon cross, still in the present churchyard, where passing monk preachers might address the local people and baptise before a church was built.

The earliest known church in Hathersage was built by Richard Basset, son of Ralph Basset, Chancellor of England in Henry I's reign. We have seen that Richard Basset and Maude Ridel, his wife, built the Augustinian Canons' priory called Launde Abbey, in Leicestershire, sometime between 1118 and 1125. With 16 other churches, Hathersage church was founded to provide tithes to fund this monastic house. It is likely that it was built sometime after the monastic foundation and probably finished by 1135. Because of its monastic association, the priests of Hathersage church were called rectors, and we begin to know their names from 1281, a hundred and fifty years after the foundation.

At this time churches were built by itinerant groups of stonemasons, carpenters and other craftsmen whose skills were far beyond those of local people, whose only contribution might be to provide transport of local stone and timber. The funding of the venture rested with the lord or his chief lord or another patron. The keystone of a Norman arch was visible in the underground boiler room in the 1940s. Today a possible trace of the original church can be found in the base of a column in the north side of the present nave.

The traces of the early building suggest a simple 'hall' construction which was aligned with the north aisle of the present building. Nothing is known of changes to the church until 1381 when, under the supervision of Rector Richard de Bretigny of Cotton Basset, the old nave became the present north aisle and a new nave was built on its south side. There was still no tower, chancel or clerestory. Attendance at Mass was expected on the three main holy days of the Church and frequent attendance was the norm. Although parts of the baptism and marriage services began outside, there was a symbolic entry into the church, so closing it to villagers for long periods while building took place would have been unacceptable. Hathersage would have been affected by the Papal Interdict in 1208, however,

18 *A medieval gargoyle once on a church roof.*

20

19 *The chapel of Launde Abbey, the only remaining part of the old buildings (by permission of the Warden of Launde Abbey Retreat House).*

which ordered the closure of all the churches in England during the Pope's quarrel with King John. It lasted for six years.

During the 14th century frequent disputes arose between the diocese of Lichfield and Launde Abbey relating to the right of presentation of a priest to Hathersage church and to the control of its tithe income. The Bishop of Lichfield had appointed Richard de Bretigny to the living in 1381 and Thomas Downes in 1390. On each occasion the Prior of Launde complained to the King. A Royal Commission was called in 1395 to resolve the issue and it ruled that the Abbey must lose the presentation but retain certain tithes. The first vicar to arrive in 1422 under the terms of the Royal Commission's decision was Thurstan Eyre, who was related to Robert Eyre I of Padley. He found the church in a state of neglect probably due to the quarrels of the previous 52 years, when there had been nine incumbents. Between them the Eyres supervised the raising of the church roof to accommodate the new high-windowed clerestory, and the building of a south aisle with a porch to be used in marriages and baptisms. This also became the venue for business agreements. A tower, chancel and font were also added in what was a period of general refurbishment of churches all over England, reflecting the wealth and religious zeal of the time.

HADERSEGE VICAR'.

PᶦOR DE LOWNDE PATRONUS.

Dñs Robtus Hulley vicar' ibm het in coïbus annis.

	£	s.	d.
In mãfione cũ gardio & una acra terre — } — vj viij			
In oblationibus — — xiij iiij			
In pafchali rotulo — — xliij iiij	vij	xj	—
In decimis metalli plũbei iiij iij iiij			
In decimis minutˢ — — iiij iiij			
Sm̃ᵃ - - -			

DEDUCTIO.

	£	s.	d.
Unde refolut' annuatī archⁿᵒ Derbie p feenag' & pcur' - - }	—	x	vij

	£	s.	d.
De claro - -	vij	—	v
Xᵐᵃ inde - -	—	xiiij	—ob'

20 *This Valor Ecclesiasticus shows the value of Hathersage church tithes to Launde Abbey in 1535 when Thomas Cromwell assessed the wealth of monasteries prior to closing them for Henry VIII. He was given Launde Abbey later.*

When Robert Eyre died in 1459 and Joan, his wife, in 1463, Robert, their elder son, continued the work by building a chantry chapel to the east of the north aisle where Masses were to be said for their souls. The Perpendicular arches confirm its date. With the tower raised and strengthened to support a spire, so fashionable about 1500, the medieval church was complete. The further refurbishments belong to a later period and some of the features of the earlier church have been obscured by them. In the 16th century, the Parish Church of St Michael and All Angels, and its people, faced new problems in the forms of the Reformation, the printed English Bible and the changes imposed upon them by the Tudors.

Chapter 7

Monastic Granges of the Derwent Valley

While the parish church of Hathersage originally existed to fund Launde Abbey through its tithes, other monasteries in the 12th century received land in and around the manor and parish of Hathersage to establish granges for monastic husbandry. The practice was to develop stock or arable farm settlements, each grange following the farming economy characteristic of its order. While some orders established labour-intensive home farms near the monastery, others preferred to assart or develop marginal land on the high moors and woodlands north of Hathersage and Hope. The grange might be attended by no more than a few shepherds or peasant cultivators inspected by lay brothers visiting on a regular or occasional basis. They sold their beasts at the new local markets coming into existence in the 1200s, and the mother house carefully counted the profit together with tithes and other income.

All granges received their land from the lord of the manor or territory. In neighbouring areas, William Peveril gave land to Lenton Priory which became known as Monksdale in 1108. Gilbert de Stoke granted half of Abney to the Cistercians of Rufford Abbey by 1201. Offerton was still part of Abney Grange under the Abbot of Rufford in 1473, the year Ralph Eyre leased land there from the abbey.

In the late 12th century Prince John, as Earl of Mortain, granted some of his woodland and moors to the west of the Derwent boundary of Hathersage to the Premonstratensian Canons of Welbeck Abbey, lands which included Ashop, Cruchill and

21 *Grange land on the upper reaches of the River Derwent.*

23

Lockerbrook right up to Derwent Head. The only condition in the charter was that 'between mid April and 24 July, the Canons should keep their cattle away from the nesting places of the earl's sparrow hawks'. The grant was reaffirmed in 1215, close to the end of John's reign, but reserving more royal rights on wood and venison, while in 1251 his son Henry III granted the monks five more acres of assart land 'in our forest of Cruchill' and the right to cut timber for building. In later years William de Ferrers, Earl of Derby, himself lord there for a time, also granted land between the River Ashop and Derwent Head.

In the early 13th century Matthew de Hathersage gave pastureland to the east of the River Derwent, within his own manor of Hathersage, to Welbeck Abbey. It included 'land for grazing in Onemansfield for eighty beasts in his forest of Hathersage'. His descendant, Oliver de Longford, with the agreement of Simon de Gousil reaffirmed the arrangement towards the end of the 13th century. His charter states that, 'Welbeck is to have in free alms for the good of his soul, one place of meadow in my forest of Hathersage which is called Onemansfield through those various markers, ditches and fences, which Master Matthew of Hathersage and I, the said Oliver, have then held *in toto*, without any other restriction.' In Mary Tudor's reign, Onemansfield house, 'formerly belonging to the Priory [*sic*] of Welbeck', was sold to Robert Barber and the name reappears, sometimes as 'Onemonksfield', in the copies of later Perambulations of the Manor.

In Edward III's reign (1327-77) there was an attempt by Welbeck Abbey to gain exemption for Cruchill Grange from a royal tithe on its 'newly tilled lands which monks have planted with vegetables with their own hands, on the increase of animals, on the gardens and on the orchards'. By then the community of labourers and lay monks had a tannery, bake house, brewhouse, forges and animal pens. While large flocks and herds were maintained, the Crown objected to the rearing of horses and many abbots throughout the woodlands and moors of their granges in the Peak were fined and banned from doing so. The name of Marebottom within Cruchill Grange suggests that the clandestine breeding of horses might have been going on at some time.

22 *The River Derwent is now dammed. In drought parts of the old village of Derwent can be seen. It once had a bridge to King John's land and the grange on the west side of the river.*

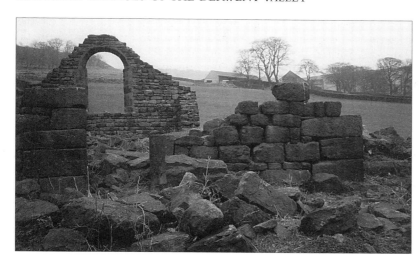

23 *An old chapel of passage or oratory for monastic travellers en route to a grange. It was later associated with North Lees Hall.*

None of the local simply-built grange buildings, lodges and booths survives from the period. It was not customary to build chapels for grange farms as monasteries avoided the expense. Yet some chapels did exist and the parish church feared the loss to them of alms and worshippers who worked for the monks. Church policy finally established that worship and alms of parishioners was not available to the grange chapels. J.C. Cox in his work on Derbyshire churches thought there were four chapels around the higher Derwent Valley, one seemingly in the village of Derwent. The existence of the other three relies on later place-names and a misunderstanding of grange communities which seldom included a priest to say Mass. It would not be unreasonable to have monastic lodges in the wild inhospitable forests of Derwent Head which served at times as oratories for private prayer and did not need a costly royal licence.

As the diocese of Lichfield grew in power and prestige, King John (1199-1216) granted it authority over the churches of Hope, Bakewell and Tideswell. By 1395 Hathersage had come under the control of the diocese, which had asserted its authority in previous years. The monasteries with remote granges in the area had to insist on their tithes, the monks of Lenton Priory breaking into Tideswell church, attacking the priest and taking sheep from the land. In Edale the Abbot of Lenton was confronted by the dangerous James Coterel acting for the chapter of Lichfield. Gradually the supervision of remote granges became too cumbersome for monasteries, who ceased to employ local labourers to work with lay monks and began to farm out parcels of land to lay tenants. The records of the Duchy of Lancaster in the 15th century list the lease values and names of tenants of Cruchill (later Crookhill) Grange.

At the Dissolution of the Monasteries in the 1530s Hathersage church was attached to Lichfield diocese, but its value was calculated in the assessment of Launde Abbey which was acquired by Thomas Cromwell, the perpetrator of the dissolutions under Henry VIII. The Cavendish family bought Cruchill Grange and the woodlands once belonging to Welbeck Abbey. In Hathersage Manor, as we have seen, Onemansfield and other monastic land was sold off in Mary Tudor's reign. Later it was part of the wastes and commons of the manor redistributed under the Enclosure Award of 1830. In the 20th century reservoirs covered the lower grange fields on the hillsides of the River Derwent. An area that always required attention and husbandry on a large scale has became a place of beauty thanks to the protection offered by Water Companies and the Peak District National Park. King John would still find a refuge for his sparrow hawks.

Chapter 8

Thieves and Rogues

Although there are different regional connections in the Midlands with Robin Hood, there is a strong tradition that he lived for a time in the Hathersage area. Local landmarks bear his name, such as Robin Hood's Cross on Abney Moor, Robin Hood's Stoop above Callow on Offerton Moor and others near the modern dams. Robin Hood's Cave on Stanage Edge is a run of linked caves.

Folklore has it that Little John lived in the area. The Longshaw estate has its Little John Well and local speculation in the early 19th century identified a stone hovel as his, although it would actually have been made of timber and impacted mud or cobs and collapsed, as did all other cottages of the medieval period, within ten to fifteen years of building.

In the churchyard, however, rests the so-called Little John's Grave, large enough to accommodate his famous height, and when the grave was opened in the 18th century a large thighbone was found. That persuades some that the 17th-century record of bow, armour and forester's cap, which were hung in the church, all belonged to him. Bowmen did not wear the superfluous chest armour and it is more likely that the bow and cap were symbols of office belonging to the Eyre family, who held the not unimportant office of Foresters in the Royal Forest of the Peak. It is interesting that the cap and bow only came to notice after the Reformation: the significance of the insignia could have been forgotten by the later Eyre family or simply attributed by the village to a safer and less politically sensitive time in the past.

Doubt has long existed as to the authenticity of Little John's Grave. One theory is that the posts at each end of the plot were originally meant to provide standard measurements of length. Their position outside the door was common in other areas at a time when business deals were often clinched outside the church, a custom now largely forgotten. It is not impossible, however, that a body was laid to rest between the posts in later times and the length of the grave has been changed more than once.

There are other difficulties about the legend. If Robin Hood had been active in the reigns of Richard I and King John, as the story has it, legal and royal records of that period are quite adequate to detail his offences, but they do not. The actual name of the evil sheriff is never mentioned in the story but the names of sheriffs were recorded as far back as 1135, holding responsibility as they did for both Nottinghamshire and Derbyshire. There were no friars in the England of King John, the first nine coming to England in 1224. The early friars were respected for their work and the concept of a self-indulgent Friar Tuck, aiding and abetting brigands in the forests, is more likely to apply to the Coterel band a hundred years later when public criticism of friars was rife.

Robin Hood was once a generic name representing defiance and independence of the law and invoking the spirit of the woods, the refuge of people fearing the unfairness of the law of the time. Tribulation certainly existed in the 13th century during hard times caused by the devaluation of currency to pay for the Welsh wars or by bad

24 *Little John was reputed to have been buried in this grave in Hathersage churchyard.*

harvests or murraines among cattle. Shortages of food led people to take to the forests, stealing, poaching and attacking travellers there with cudgels which gave them the later name of trailbastons. A century after the Robin Hood legend, there was a very real bandit operating in the Peak. James Coterel came from a family holding land near the Derbyshire and Staffordshire border. He led a band of brigands which, together with similar trailbaston bands elsewhere, terrorised the Midlands from 1320 to 1333. He and his brothers formed alliances with Roger le Sauvage, whose manor was in Sherwood Forest area, the Folvilles of Ashby Folville in Leicestershire and the Bradburns in Yorkshire, who had a henchman who was 'a certain John the Little'.

Hathersage lay in the zone of Coterel's movements and was in the path of sorties to the east to meet associates. The chief lord of Hathersage, Roger de Bellers, was murdered by the Folvilles near his Leicestershire manor in retaliation for his investigation, ordered by the chief justices, into attacks on property. It would be a lesser Hathersage lord, Nicholas de Longford, who finally helped to curtail their activities in 1333 as one of the law officers in a Commission of Trailbaston appointed by the Crown.

Coterel and his lieutenants were themselves minor landed gentry and some were tenants of the Royal Duchy of Lancaster in the Peak. In spite of his activities James was able to obtain the wardship of a rich widow at Tideswell. His younger brother, Nicholas, was for a time the bailiff of Edward III's Queen Philippa, a major landowner in the Peak. He was also active as a gang member and had enough standing to buy a Basset girl as a bride.

The Coterel gang attracted men of many ranks united in their antipathy to the Duchy of Lancaster and won the sympathies of highborn gentry who sometimes hired them for private raids. Coterel's evil genius was a priest called Robert Bernard, who had a background of imprisonment for intrigue with Edward II's Queen Isabella; after his release he was suspected of involvement in the murder of Edward II in 1327. Bernard had been a sometime clerk in Chancery, a university teacher at Oxford, vicar of a Rutland parish and latterly a Canon and Registrar of the Chapter of Lichfield Cathedral, in which diocese the Peak and many of the Lancaster estates lay. Now he incited James Coterel and his followers to develop their life of crime, lending them his support from within the cathedral chapter. Bernard had designs on Bakewell parish and had himself installed as vicar in 1327 only to antagonise the parishioners so much that on Christmas Day 1327 they stripped him of his eucharistic vestments and ejected him from the church (Acta Capitularum Lichfield folio 22). He remained vicar, however, and went on to embezzle the income of Bakewell parish church. On 1 June 1328 the Bishop of Lichfield was commanded by papal mandate to remove him from Bakewell but he was still causing trouble in August when, on his instigation, James, John and Nicholas Coterel

together with Roger le Sauvage and others 'threw
down Walter Cam, Vicar of Bakewell and took ten
shillings from the offerings'.

It was difficult for Edward II's ministers to restore
law and order. Juries were intimidated. The General
Eyre of July 1330 met at Derby to get to the bottom
of the disorder and the murders of the recent years
but it came to nothing. Kidnap and menaces continued
to raise money 'ad opus societatis', plainly the *cosa
nostra* of the Coterels.

The Coterels ignored summons to the courts
but by 20 March 1331 they were on the run and
outlawed. From then on for the next eighteen months
the gang rampaged and robbed through the Peak.
More justices had been commissioned as a result of
the Commission of Trailbaston in the spring of 1332,
a court consisting of, among others, the Chief Justice
of the King's Bench and Nicholas Longford, lesser lord
of Hathersage. The judges and justices held sessions all
over the north Midlands and their effectiveness was
a turning point. By now Coterel, still an attractive
figure to some, was reduced to wandering in the
Peak with 20 followers. It is almost certain that they
sheltered in the caves near Castleton, five miles west
of the Hathersage parish border, and there is a later
folk memory of a certain Cock Lorel who hid there.
Somehow the Robin Hood legend and the Coterel
saga have become interwoven. Coterel's associates
in Yorkshire, the Bradburns, had a henchman called

25 *Roger de Bellers after his murder
lies in Kirby Bellars church. This print
is dated 1790. The figures date from
the death of his mother c.1360.*

John the Little; the bankrupt De Sauvage had lost his inheritance in Sherwood, forcing
him to become a bandit.

By the summer of 1332 the concerted effort of the Commission of Trailbaston
and the new Justices had begun to bear fruit. Rehabilitating some pardoned members
and isolating others broke up the gang. The Crown won back the loyalty of disaffected
and impecunious knights by employing them on military campaigns. Many had been
in service before and had joined the gang because of debt or some grudge regarding
title or property. Robert Bernard of Lichfield made a plea of 'benefit of the clergy' and
avoided secular penalty. He went back to Oxford and helped establish the abortive new
university at Stamford. Through January to March 1333 the work of the court continued
with a steady stream of followers hauled before the justices. The Coterels never stood trial:
Nicholas was selected to lead 60 men to the wars in Scotland but he appropriated their
pay fund and disappeared; James Coterel, still in touch with Lichfield Cathedral, went
on to become an administrator for the Crown. His associates, the Foljambes, Gresleys
and Bradburns, would become respected landed gentry within a few years.

It is no coincidence that the Coterel gang thrived in the last unhappy years of
Edward II's reign when administration of law was uncertain. The breakdown of feudal
obedience was always more likely when the Crown was distracted. In time Edward III
and his advisors broke the power of the criminal band, although the problem of social
disorder would be resurrected in a new guise after the Black Death less than twenty
years later.

Chapter 9

The Manor of Hathersage

In Domesday Book Hathersage included Hurst, Bamford and Derwent, half of Offerton and two parts of Stoney Middleton. Padley was not listed as a manor in its own right and its land north of Wath Brook belonged to Hathersage. As in other manors, periodic perambulations were made to inspect and define the boundaries. In the case of Hathersage the parish limits followed the manorial boundaries although not without monastic complexities in the Derwent woodlands. Village jurors and agents of the lord would walk and ride along the boundaries, which were often brooks and watercourses, and list the names of distinctive landmarks which changed little over time.

The Perambulation of 1656, necessary because of the sale of the Fitzherbert lordship and land, was only one of many. The starting point was Abbey Bank at the junction of the River Derwent and Abbey Brook and it continued,

> One Man's House ... alias Abbey, following the wall to Carr Bank to ... Holden, Derwent to the top of Lord's Seat Hill ... to the top of the mountain to North Wain Stones ... to the water at Dovestones Torr following the water falling west and south to Brownclough Knowl and the water at Rising Clough Ridge ... to Hamblestone Cross alias Moscar thence to the top of the mountain to Stannage Edge ... Broad Rake ... Torr Top to Crow Chin ... along the water near Great Hull and Little Hull ... Fryer Ridge, Fryer Moss ... along the water into Burbage to the eight stones near Oxstones ... as far as the water falleth into said rivulet of Burbage ... to Fingeram Stone standing on the east side of the way from Sheffield to Grindleford Bridge ... which said stone parteth the Hundred of High Peak and Scardale as well as the manors of Hathersage and Dore. Thence to Strawberry Lee Knave on the west side of Totley Moss, north to White Edge ... to Lady Cross to said Edge as the water falleth by Hurkling Stone and then to Hinley Well that parteth the Manor of Hathersage and Baslow to Wath Brook alias Rash Brook which runs into said rivulet of Burbadge into the River Derwent to Hurst Clough Brook to Reeve Side up to the Standing Stone on to Moscar and Howden Brook into Chibbage or Lady Bower Brook where it runneth into the said River Derwent at Abbey.

It is interesting that Bamford, an outlier of the manor of Hathersage in Domesday Book, was separated at some time in the Middle Ages and became a sub-manor. The Inquisition Post Mortem of 1355, after Elizabeth Furnival's death, stated that the manor of Bamford belonging to the lord of Hathersage was held for her in dower as widow of Sir Thomas Furnival, at a rent of 12 pence a year with boon service. Stoney Middleton was another outlier to go its own way, except for the curacy held by the vicar of Hathersage until the 19th century. The migration of the Ashton family from Stoney Middleton in the 17th century also provided another link.

The 1792 Perambulation of jurors made 'by order of Mr Eadon, steward to the Duke of Devonshire' found the boundaries little changed. They remained the same on

26 *Boundaries of Hathersage Manor in 1656.*

the large maps made by the commissioners of the Hathersage Enclosure of Wastes and Commons between 1808 and 1830 who proposed new enclosures of the old common land and wastes separating the townships of Hathersage and Padley. Although Padley must not be ignored in a study of Hathersage manor, it is atypical in that it was shared with Baslow manor and had a different economy, with at least two lead mills working in the Middle Ages.

27 *Lady Elizabeth Montacute, granddaughter of Simon de Montfort. As widow of her second husband, Thomas Furnival, she was tenant of the Longford lords of Hathersage for land in Bamford. She became patroness of St Frideswide's nunnery in Oxford and is buried in the chancel of Christ Church, originally the convent's church. She preferred to use the title from her first marriage. She died in 1354. The figures decorating her tomb were defaced in a later period.*

The early medieval village of Hathersage lay close to its church and away from the flood plain of the River Derwent, near the Dale with its springs and brook. The location of Matthew de Hathersage's messuage mentioned in the document of 1263 is not known but we know of Elizabeth Furnival's boon service as tenant of the Longford lords of Hathersage, which was to provide men for a day's labour at haymaking.

Place-names give clues as to farming practice. At some time Townfield was a large open field west of the track called Booth Lane (now Sheffield Road), up to the height of 700 feet or below. Its 12 to 15 ft wide strips or 'lands' can occasionally be seen in snowlines and Ninelands Road reminds us of a set of strips which lay together measuring the usual furlong in length. Fields bearing the name of 'dole' recalled the measuring sticks used by the manorial court to supervise the measurement of strips. Baulk Lane, a name found in many villages, defines the edge of another great open field. Snowlines can also show strip divisions high above Seel Field and east of the present Sheffield Road; these were cultivated in times of famine, poor climate or increased population, and abandoned later. It is rarely possible to see in Hathersage the contours of 13th-century strips as later cultivation overlaid them. What we see are mostly the 15th-century field lines or the last arable cultivation before a field was put down to pasture.

Few manorial court records for Hathersage survive before 1656 but the later records include topics familiar in other manors in the Middle Ages: fallow fields were determined for the season, grazing areas were defined and designated and open arable fields were opened to cattle and sheep at specified times and dates each year. Large animals were kept out of the village fields by fencing or hedges but were let in after the last harvest to graze and add manure to the fields. The existing Pinfold at the bottom of the Dale reminds us of the need for a pen for straying animals. Herdsmen tending their stock in severe weather used booths or huts often on the outskirts of villages of the Hope Valley

29 *Snowlines on Townfield define old strips.*

and the name persists at the edges of Hathersage and Edale in an area where, in 1255, wolves were still a threat to man and beast.

Herds were diminished in winter because of lack of feed. Meat was not eaten regularly because preservation was expensive. Cumin was grown and important tenants, like Robert Eyre in 1506, had to provide as part of the rent to their overlords a pound of cumin seed, which was valued as a strong flavouring to hide the taste of long-stored meat.

The manor of Baslow met that of Hathersage at Padley and its manorial court records are extant from 1319. It is possible to discern the frustrations of Lord Vernon of Baslow at the encroachments of so-called free tenants and well-born tenants of high rank. There is a break in the records for some years after the Black Death of 1349-55 and afterwards the breakdown of feudal law becomes apparent. There is anger that Robert Eyre of Hathersage, in the pay of the Earl of Shrewsbury, was moving lead and millstones across the moor and manor boundaries, and that an Eyre had built a weir without the lord's permission.

In Baslow the lord ordered the rebuilding of derelict houses and gave permission for the timber and best cob to be taken to make the daub and wattle dwellings which had an oven in a hut outside. Roofs were thatched, for anything heavier would have caused the walls to collapse. If Little John had a dwelling in the village it is long gone.

Chapter 10

The Eyres of Hathersage

The stories surrounding the Eyres of Padley are numerous and reveal more about attitudes of later writers than they do about the medieval family. The Eyres merit attention not for their supposed military exploits but as a vigorous and industrious local family in the Middle Ages. This long-lasting family survived the Black Death and only lost its identity when, in the 18th century, descendants in the direct male line adopted the surnames of Archer, Newton and Gell after they married.

The Eyres appear in Chancery documents, charters, tax valuations, land claims and property inventories at family deaths. Although there were three Robert Eyres of Padley in the 15th century, in the parish church of Hathersage, which they enlarged, there is only one tomb, that of Robert Eyre I and Joan his wife; there are two other brass tablets which are not contemporary with Eyre deaths, and they have been moved at least once. There are no parish registers to help us before 1627 and the Herald's Visitations of 1569 and 1611 are not very accurate, relying heavily on oral tradition.

The Eyre family was living in Hope by 1305, when a Robert Eyre witnessed a land grant. His descendants are mentioned in legal documents many times during the 14th century. In the early 1400s a Robert Eyre was referred to as a 'forester', an official of the Royal Forest of the Peak. The family status can be judged from an entry in the Plumpton Deeds of 1335 when 'Nicholas, son of Robert Eyre of Hope, was granted rents, customs, and suit of court in the lordship of Thornhill'.

30 *Robert Eyre I d.1459 and Joan Padley his wife.*

In 1408, however, the Eyres were in trouble with the law and summoned to appear before King Henry IV in Chancery. It was recorded in the Patent Rolls on 11 January that Robert Eyre the Younger had kidnapped Joan, daughter and heiress of the deceased Nicholas Padley. Cecily, her mother, appealed to the King for justice. The King commissioned three men, Roger Leach, Thomas Foljeamp (Foljambe) and John Stafford, to arrest Robert Eyre the Elder (the father), William Abney of Hope, Robert Eyre the Younger and Nicholas his brother, John Balge (Balguy) of Aston and William Eyre of Thornhill. All were to be held until they offered security that they would appear before the King in Chancery at the Easter session to answer to the King and to Joan's family. They were also to be held until they delivered Joan up and she was then to be kept safely and 'this was to be certified to the king'.

The trial never happened but the marriage of Robert the Younger with Joan Padley took place in

1408-9. He is now referred to as Robert Eyre I of Padley, and the marriage was to last 50 years and produce 15 children. The family lived at Padley Hall, within the manor and parish of Hathersage, two miles down river from the church of St Michael.

It is possible that, as legend has it, Robert Eyre I fought at the Battle of Agincourt in 1415 with a band of local men. There is a list of 1416 in which the names of two Eyres appear, but the purpose of this list is unclear because all the other Agincourt muster lists are dated 1415. This may have been a local muster unit on standby and never called. The record itself may have been made after the men had served but this cannot be proved. Robert Eyre I of Padley was certainly not knighted at any time.

31 *Robert Eyre II, died c.1500, and his wife, Elizabeth Fitz William.*

What is more clearly documented is a murder charge against a Robert Eyre of Padley in 1429. The Kings' Justices, Peter Pole and Gerard Meynil, in court at Derby heard the case against him on 25 April 1430, and before the King's Coroner, John Dunbaben, he was accused of the murder of William Woodrove of Hope, gentleman. Evidence heard during the trial produced the following facts. The two men were riding from Chesterfield to Holme on Sunday after the Feast of Holy Cross in the eighth year of Henry VI's reign, or 19 September 1429. The annual Chesterfield Fair was being held at this time and it is possible that they were returning home from it. There are many places called Holme in the Chesterfield area but since Robert Eyre would be heading for Padley and Woodrove (or Woodruff) for Hope, their destination was very likely to be the Holme Hall at Brampton, which was an Eyre residence. William Woodrove became quarrelsome, both men dismounted from their horses and Woodrove, drawing his sword, hit Robert on the back of the head. 'Only the large red kerchief wound several times round my head saved my life,' Robert alleged. This kerchief would resemble the scarf of a 'liripipe', a variation of the roundlet headgear fashionable at that time. Robert then fended off William and hid in a hedge but was trapped there. He hit William on the head with his sword and wounded him mortally, William lingering speechless for two days before he died. The outcome of the trial was that the jury declared Robert Eyre of Padley 'not guilty' although the events as cited suggest otherwise. But Eyre's status and his local, influential friends suggest this was a safe verdict for a jury to give.

32 *Sketch showing the liripipe, a forerunner of the roundlet, which saved Eyre's life in 1429.*

33 *Offerton Hall, once the home of Robert Eyre's brother, Ralph Eyre d.1493. He was tenant of Abney Grange. The Hall was extended in the Elizabethan period.*

The problem to consider is whether father or son was the defendant. Robert Eyre I was by 1429 a family man thirty to forty years old. Robert Eyre II was a young man about twenty years old. The incident seems more likely to be a fracas between young men returning from the heady pastimes of the fair, but we will never know.

The Eyres were men of business with interests in the local lead industry and quarrying. In 1442, when Thurstan Eyre became vicar of Hathersage parish, Robert I was enlarging and refurbishing the church as previously described. The Eyres were benefactors of the church, as the Longfords had never been in their time as lesser lords. Robert Eyre I, assessed at 100 shillings in the Derbyshire tax inquisitions of 1431, had the wealth and resources to make this building project possible and the devotion to execute it.

There is an extant cashbook of 1466 relating to the Yarncliff millstone quarry in Hathersage belonging to Robert Eyre II of Padley. It records his two brothers and the names of his workmen and their wages as well as receipts from the sales of pairs of millstones and orders from customers. The Eyres had interests in other quarries in Hathersage parish, on Stanage and Millstone Edges, the latter rented by Nicholas Eyre in 1475, and the transformation of the church owed much to these quarries and the businesses of the Eyres, notwithstanding their other commitments as property owners in Hope and Eyam.

Robert Eyre I of Padley died in 1459 and Joanne of Padley, his wife, in 1463. Their heir, Robert II, added a chantry chapel to the church where Mass would be said for his parents' souls by a chantry priest paid by him. He also installed the Sanctus Bell, dedicated to their memory, in the new church tower. The spire is of about 1500 and more likely the work of his son, Robert III.

Robert Eyre II married Elizabeth Fitz William, daughter of Thomas Fitz William of Mablethorpe, one time Steward of the Duchy of Lancaster. Robert and Elizabeth Eyre are depicted in memorial brasses in Hathersage church which have been moved and reset more than once. The faces are young, the hair and shoe styles are late 15th century, but the tabard belongs to a later convention in brasses of the 1500s. As so often is the case, the brasses were not contemporary with the demise of the couple in about 1500. Four of their sons kneel behind them although they had many more children and Robert the heir is not included. It may well be that the children on the brass predeceased their parents or had died by the time the brass was commissioned. Robert Eyre II lived to a great age and was still conducting business until at least 1496, when he was described as 'the Elder' to distinguish him from his son Robert Eyre III who was 'the Younger'. They worked in business and public life at the same time and both their names sometimes appear on the same document. One of them was a Sheriff of Derbyshire in 1480 but we cannot know which one.

Robert III (the Younger) married Elizabeth, daughter of Nicholas Hodelston. Their marriage settlement in Clowne Papers is dated 30 December 1471 but the marriage would follow sometime after that. Arthur, their son and heir born in 1482, was so named four years before Henry VII in 1486 gave the same name to the Prince of Wales at his birth. There is no tomb or brass in Hathersage church to commemorate Robert III, who died aged about fifty only four years after the death of his father. His son Arthur Eyre succeeded him in 1504 although the Inquisition Post Mortem for the vast and complex estate was delayed until 1506.

By the 15th century the Eyres had become agents of great families like the Plumptons, the Earl of Shrewsbury, and the Lovels, keeping a watchful eye on their clients' interests in local properties and legal affairs. In the next century they would send their sons to the Inns of Court.

Chapter 11

The Plumpton Connection

The Eyres of Padley in the 15th century were stewards or seneschals of the Plumptons of Spofforth, Yorkshire, who themselves were long-standing stewards of the great Percys, Earls of Northumberland. Sir William Plumpton had estates in Derbyshire once belonging to his mother, Alice Foljambe, the sole heiress of a wealthy Derbyshire family. The Wars of the Roses tested the vulnerability of such a family. Sir William Plumpton, loyal to King Henry VI, had many responsibilities including those of sheriff of three counties, but in 1461 his son was killed at the Battle of Towton and King Henry VI was deposed. Being a supporter of the Lancastrian cause, Plumpton was dismissed from his post of steward of the Yorkshire estates of the Duchy of Lancaster, although he was pardoned and reinstated by the Yorkist Edward IV in 1464.

Only daughters of Sir William's first marriage survived but in secret he had married again, a union later regarded as of dubious legality. Robert Plumpton (1453-1523) was born of that marriage and inherited from his father in 1480 an estate which was to be challenged as illegal. The legal dispute was to last into the next century. More trouble came from his allegiance to the Percys which led him to fight with them on the Yorkist side in the Battle of Bosworth of 1485, a fact which did not commend him to Henry VII. In 1487, however, he joined the glittering entourage of Lord Percy, who made a conciliatory visit to London to honour the new Tudor king in the queen's coronation year, and he was later knighted.

To assist him with his legal problems Sir Robert Plumpton appointed six lawyers, one of whom was Thomas Fitz William, Robert Eyre II's father or brother-in-law. When he decided to appoint two stewards to administer his Derbyshire property, one of them was Robert Eyre III of Padley. This was the period in which the feudal obligations between lord and subtenants had broken down. The Wars of the Roses had done much damage to gentry like the Plumptons, who walked a knife edge between the policies of their great lords and the royal fortunes of York and Lancaster. The gentry became retainers of great men at court and in turn built up their own faction of men of business and law to support them.

It was in this context that Robert Eyre III of Padley served Sir Robert Plumpton as steward. The connection had begun in a small way long before, the Plumptons having given a John Eyre the post of chantry priest, a poorly paid sinecure, in the Plumpton Chapel of Holy Trinity, Ripon by 1430. In the 1480s, as the plight of Sir Robert Plumpton became perilous, control over him by his new steward Robert Eyre intensified. In 1480 Sir Robert was preparing to lease the old Foljambe manor of Hassop to Stephen Eyre, Robert's brother. In 1489 Robert wrote to his 'master' Plumpton reporting a property dispute and asked for letters of attorney to deal with the matter. By 1500 Eyre had made an even firmer connection with the Plumptons, his son and heir Arthur, aged 18 years, having contracted to marry Sir Robert's daughter, Margaret, by 4 August. Letters of 1501 and 1503 show that Margaret, who may have been much the younger, continued to live with her own family after the marriage. The tone of Robert Eyre's letters changes about then, as he gives advice to 'my right worshipful brother' with the assurance of an equal.

The Plumpton inheritance dispute had escalated into intricate land quarrels by 1501, attracting the unwelcome attention of the great courtier Empson who intimidated judges by his attendance with retainers at assize courts. This type of interference with law courts was not uncommon and in 1504 Henry VII was to ban the practice of 'maintenance' and the keeping of retainers in private livery in great households. Meanwhile Plumpton's anxiety continued. Sir Robert sought the good offices of the Earl of Shrewsbury, who was not proving easy to meet. In a letter of June 1501 he wants to meet Shrewsbury and will 'pick up Robert Eyre on the way to Wingfield'. In September Eyre wrote to him of the difficulty in knowing the venue of the court they were to attend, as the King had assembled all his justices for a meeting. Eyre had been looking for jury support, especially in the High Peak, and persuading witnesses for the rival claimants not to appear at a forthcoming hearing. He is surprised that Plumpton has not taken up lodging available for his supporters in Derby as Empson has 'taken much lodging in Derby' where the case might be heard.

In September 1502 Empson appeared at York Assizes with 200 knightly gentlemen and yeomen where Sir Robert Plumpton's case concerning his Yorkshire properties was being heard before a packed jury. Plumpton lost his case, was imprisoned for a time and only later was able to repossess his manor of Plumpton. The family was ruined, although some of its estates were retrieved by descendants like the Clifford relations, from whom the Eyres of Hassop would hold leases in the future.

For Robert Eyre the Plumpton marriage was a lasting prize linking his son with a knightly family and an illustrious Foljambe ancestor. In addition he had become Seneschal of the Earl of Shrewsbury. His high-handed acts on behalf of this master are recorded in the Baslow Court rolls. In 1483 the Earl and his Seneschal had held two courts of usurpation in Baslow although the Earl was only a free tenant in that manor. The same year there was a complaint that 'R. Eyre makes drives (of beasts) on the moor contrary to the rights and titles and his heirship of Hope Valley'. The Eyres of Padley were clearly poor neighbours and tenants, establishing weirs, gathering wood and bracken without necessary licence and ignoring manorial rights of others over the moors.

They were involved not only with the Plumptons and Shrewsbury but also the Lovels of Holmesfield. Court rolls of 1480-1 reveal that Robert Eyre esquire was 'seneschal of the manorial court' of Francis, Lord Lovel. Lovel, a great landowner with many court offices, was one of the most powerful men in England under Richard III and he is mentioned in the rhyme

> The catte, the ratte, and Lovel our dogge,
> Rule all England under the hogge.

Lovel escaped with his life after the Battle of Bosworth, which established Henry VII as King. He returned in 1487 to support Lambert Simnel's claim only to disappear again after the Battle of Stoke near Newark. This time his estates were forfeit. Holmesfield Manor was given to a soldier, John Savage, later to be knighted. He had business with Robert Eyre, who was expected at the Holmesfield manorial court but did not attend. It is interesting that in 1565, 77 years later, another Robert Eyre, gentleman of Gray's Inn, appointed two attorneys to do his business with a later lord 'in the court of Sir John Savage at his manor of Holmesfield, according to the custom of the court'. The Eyre family's advancement continued through the Wars of the Roses, unlike some of their masters.

Chapter 12

Arthur Eyre
1481-1535

Arthur Eyre was 23 years old when in November 1504 he inherited the estate of his father Robert Eyre III of Padley. The Inquisition Post Mortem, only completed on 23 July 1506, gives an exact record of the property of this wealthy landed family. The trustees of Robert's will included Thomas FitzWilliam, one of his mother's family, and close family ties reflected in the grants of land made by the earlier Robert Eyre were now reaffirmed by his son. These included grants to Richard of Plumpton, chaplain, Philip Eyre, rector of Ashover church, Roger Eyre of Holme Hall and Thomas Eyre of Highlow.

Arthur Eyre acquired hundreds of acres of land, meadow, pasture and woods as hereditary tenancies in the Peak. His overlords included the king in three different titles of lordship, three abbots of three different orders, Lichfield Cathedral, the Earl of Shrewsbury as Baron of Crich or Lord of Eyam, and two other gentlemen. For his lands he was legally required to make nine acts of fealty, perform two military services and attend eight different manorial courts twice a year. In addition, for his land in Abney, he must give cumin. While some of these feudal obligations may have been relaxed, it is well to remember that manorial courts continued until the 19th century, and a tenant in the Duchy of Lancaster could still be admonished for not grinding his corn at the king's mill.

The Eyre estates in Hathersage were numerous:

A fourth part of the manor of Hathersage, and ten messuages, 200 acres of land, 120 acres of pasture, 40 acres of meadow, 10 acres of wood, 10 shillings free rent and half a pound of cummin and a halfpenny in Hathersage, Padley, Netherpadley, Derwent, and

34 *Brass rubbing of Arthur Eyre, d.1535, and his first wife, Margaret Plumpton.*

Ashoppe; all these worth £6, held of George, Earl of Shrewsbury, as of his barony of Crich by knight service.

Two other messuages at 'Asshoppe' were separate and held under the Duchy of Lancaster.

It is extraordinary that so little else is known about Arthur Eyre. We do not know precisely when he died and no Inquisition Post Mortem has ever been found. The memorial brass tablet in Hathersage church made sometime later tells us he married three times. Margaret Plumpton was contracted to marry him in 1500 and she bore him seven children, all of whom died young except for a daughter, Anne. Arthur's second wife was Alice, daughter of Thomas Coffyn. The memorial brass says Coffyn was of 'Devonshire' but other sources refer to him as 'of Derby'. This is more likely, given that a member of the family, William Coffyn, was a Duchy commissioner and also a Sheriff of Derbyshire in 1530. Alice bore Arthur Eyre a child, George, who also died young. Arthur's third and childless marriage was to Dorothy Okeover, daughter of Humphrey Okeover of Staffordshire, a man of business in the Duchy of Lancaster.

The memorial tablet in Hathersage church has been misconstrued in the past, leading to the mistaken idea that Arthur was knighted. There is no evidence to support this in the densely packed information on the brass about his wives and children, yet his first father-in-law is carefully named as Sir Robert Plumpton, Knight. Of Arthur, however, it merely gives a symbol for 'Dominus' or Sir, a common mark of respect for a gentleman. In the *Paston Letters* the family refers to their chaplain as Sir Gloys; other examples are Sir Edward Savage, priest, and Sir John Vernon Esquire, listed as sheriff in 1523. Arthur Eyre is not listed as a knight at the College of Arms. The suggestion that he was knighted persists in the Herald's Visitation of 1611, where he is referred to as Arthur Eyre, Knight, but the earlier Visitation of 1569 was incomplete and relied heavily on families' attempts to enhance their pedigrees either for visiting clerks or in correspondence with the heralds.

THE EYRES OF PADLEY HALL

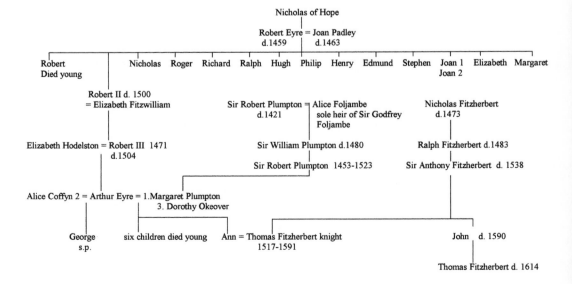

The most positive evidence of his status is in the records of the Duchy of Lancaster, whose Chancellor was the Eyres' illustrious relation by marriage, the right honourable Sir William Fitz William, Knight. Between the years 1506 and 1531 Arthur is mentioned not only in court cases in the Duchy council, but in instructions to officers and in minutes of proceedings, usually at the end of lists of names or signatories as Arthur Eyre, sometimes 'esquire'. In Henry VII's reign he became one of the tenants of the Duchy, his allocation being at Chapelside by Crookhill, and under Henry VIII the same tenancy was renewed. He appears as plain Arthur Eyre on land leases and also in his lease as collector of the 'lot and cope', the royal lead duty, from lead mills in the High Peak.

In 1516 Arthur was one of the commissioners of the Duchy to enquire about the overstocking of land in the High Peak whose report states, 'we John Wellys and Arthur Eyre have been to the King's Forest'. He was in another commission of 1525-6. In 1528 the parties to a court case involving a long dispute between the Abbot of Leicester and tenants at Over Haddon were instructed to 'abide by the arbitration and judgement of William Cossyn and Arthur Eyre, esquires'. A further petition by the Abbot of Leicester in 1531 makes the last known reference in connection with the Duchy of Lancaster to 'Arthur Eyre, esquire'. In a Chancery Feet of Fines of 1533 drafted at Westminster he was still Arthur Eyre, esquire. Finally, in a document of 20 October 1535 in which his trustees transferred his lands to his daughter Anne and her husband after his death, he was styled simply as 'Arthur Eyre'.

Chapter 13

Sir Thomas Fitzherbert
1517-1591

Hathersage was to come into the public eye under the lordship of Sir Thomas Fitzherbert, a leading recusant. Arthur Eyre's prestige as a landowner and commissioner of the Duchy of Lancaster enabled him to make a good match for his only surviving daughter. With Anthony Fitzherbert, of the great Staffordshire family, he agreed the conditions of the intended marriage of Anne Eyre and Thomas Fitzherbert when they were still children. Eyre could have expected the protection of his daughter's inheritance under the wing of her future father-in-law, the great lawyer who in 1525 would become Sir Anthony Fitzherbert and Justice in the Court of Common Pleas. In the trustees' document of 20 October 1535, the marriage had already taken place and Arthur was dead; it affirmed Arthur Eyre's estate and handed over the responsibility for it to Thomas and Anne.

Anne features little in the record but must be pitied as the lonely sole survivor of her siblings, subject to two stepmothers, whose husband's recusancy would lead to persecution in the future. Thomas Fitzherbert had acquired his wife's inheritance but the couple may not have occupied Padley, preferring the Norbury and Hamstall Ridware estates which he inherited in 1538. Thomas allowed his younger brother John to live at Padley Hall some time after 1538. He was knighted with other gentlemen, including George Talbot, the future 6th Earl of Shrewsbury and later one of his persecutors, during the celebrations of the coronation of Edward VI, on 22 February 1546/7. (The New Year began on Lady Day 25 March but modern reckoning will be used from now on.)

Sir Thomas Fitzherbert, lord of so many other manors elsewhere, was to become lord of the manor of Hathersage. The marriage with Anne Eyre did not make him so, as his deceased father-in-law was merely a tenant of the chief lord. Already holding land in Hathersage, Sir Thomas had been one of a long line of trustees administering it on behalf of the Longfords before the manor was sold to Sir William Holles in 1537. A manorial court roll of 1547 states that the Hathersage court baron was held in the names of Sir Thomas Holles and Sir Thomas Fitzherbert together.

It must have been in a state of high optimism that Sir Thomas Fitzherbert added to his wife's quarter of Hathersage by buying the Holles half of Hathersage in 1551. Sir William Holles, who had bought Hathersage from Ralph Longford in 1537, was a wealthy mercer and entrepreneur with three wool houses in Calais as well as property scattered in many parts of England. He was Lord Mayor of London in 1540 and had been intent on building up a dynasty of high manorial status but died by 1543 and his estates were divided among his three sons. The manors of Hathersage, Barlborough and Killamarsh came to his eldest son, Sir Thomas Holles. In the *Memorials of the Holles Family* in 1658 Gervase Holles describes how decayed Sir William's memorial in St Helen's Church, Bishopsgate in London was. He goes on to say that Sir Thomas Holles was a wastrel, married to a lady at court with expensive tastes who squandered his fortune, and he had to sell much of his inheritance. This included Hathersage and in 1551 Holles sold the old Longford moiety to Sir Thomas Fitzherbert, who now became lord of the manor.

In 1555 Sir Thomas Fitzherbert bought the old Gousill portion from the Thorps, now of Danethorp, thus unifying Hathersage for the first time since the 13th century. By now Sir Thomas had been appointed sheriff in Staffordshire three times, in 1546, the last year of Henry VIII's reign, again in Edward VI's first regnal year, and then in 1554 in Mary Tudor's reign.

A private sadness must have been that no children were born to the marriage of Thomas Fitzherbert and Anne Eyre. The date of Anne's death is unknown but with it the Padley Eyres' connection with Hathersage, lasting some one hundred and sixty years, came to an end. It may have been Anne's death that triggered the arrangements which Sir Thomas made in 1574 for the succession of his nephew Thomas as his heir in the event of the death of himself and his brother John.

By then national events had changed his life. After the accession of Elizabeth I in 1558 Sir Thomas's worst fears for Catholics were realised by the Act of Supremacy and Act of Uniformity in 1559. Penalties for recusancy, or refusal to attend a church service using the Book of Common Prayer, were put in place, but the new laws were seldom put into practice for the Queen was aware that older people born in her father's reign were probably all baptised as Catholics. In the hills of Derbyshire most people were still worshipping in the Catholic faith. A report to the Privy Council from the Earl of Shrewsbury in August 1588 indicates that hardly anyone ever attended the Anglican service in Hathersage. No fines were recorded for recusancy until 1581, when a stricter enforcement of the law was ordered, and the outcome was that a few retainers attached to the Padley estate were fined at the Derby Assizes in 1581.

While other courtiers and aristocrats, like William Cecil and George Talbot, the Earl of Shrewsbury, survived the royal changes of religious policy in the previous Tudor reigns

35 *All that remains of the medieval Padley Hall. Used as a farm building until the 1930s, the gatehouse is now a Catholic chapel.*

by bowing gracefully to them, Sir Thomas Fitzherbert decided to make a stand for his Catholic faith. The Queen's councillors, faced with his defiance as early as 1563, trod warily, remembering the religious vicissitudes of the last 16 years. In a letter to William Cecil, the Bishop of London described Fitzherbert as uncompromisingly 'stiff'. He wrote that Sir Thomas had been offered liberty on sureties if he would at least agree to attend church without receiving communion, but Sir Thomas had twice refused the offer. What seemed to develop over the years was a situation whereby the statutory fines and some sort of imprisonment were imposed on the recusant who, when released, resumed his stand and incurred a repetition of the penalties. His prisons except the last are not known but it was not uncommon for a man of his quality to be put under house arrest with a conforming and trusted Protestant, or confined in some comfort in lodgings close to a prison. He was able to receive and write letters, to influence his manorial court and to run his affairs in Padley and other estates by relying on his agents, his attorneys and his brother John, who was at liberty at Padley Hall.

He was still able to raise money for the fines from the rents of his tenant farmers. He also had valuable lead mining and smelting interests in Derbyshire. Some time before 1585 Sir Thomas built a lead smelting mill on the rushing Burbage Brook, a few hundred yards from Padley Hall. In 1585 the west end of the mill was let to two tenants for 18 years with use of the trees and underwood necessary as fuel for smelting. He also granted them a 21-year sub-lease to collect one half of the 'lot and cope' of the High Peak. Just as his father-in-law, Arthur Eyre, had obtained from the Crown the role of collector or 'farmer' of lead duties, called 'lot and cope', so Fitzherbert had also bought the concession in the High Peak, a lucrative source of income for the holder. Although records are not complete for this period, it seems that he still had the concession to 'farm' at his death in 1591 but was not able to organise the collection of dues remaining to him. In 1615-16 an inquiry noted that the mine office was run down and decayed, measuring of lead had not been carried out, and the farmer's right to pre-emption of lead had fallen into disuse.

Although vulnerable to Catholic plots after her excommunication by the Pope in 1570, Queen Elizabeth maintained her policy of moderation until the Act in 1581 which imposed heavy fines and imprisonment for recusancy. It seems not to have been effective and several plots to put Catholic Mary Queen of Scots on the English throne were discovered. With the assassination in the Netherlands in 1584 of the Protestant William the Silent fresh in public memory, Queen Elizabeth's parliament passed anti-recusant legislation in 1585 against Jesuit priests working in England, reinforcing this with an Act in 1587 which enabled the Crown to seize two-thirds of a recusant's land and all his goods on the non-payment of the £20 fine. The Privy Council were to supervise the application of the Act. The effects of it fell heavily on Sir Thomas Fitzherbert, who as early as 1580 had been on William Cecil's county lists of recusants, having 'a dwelling in Caulke Woods in Derbyshire, his house is a common harbour for all priests'. He had difficulty in raising the money to pay the fines necessary to save them from escheat and was imprisoned. He had already anticipated that his estates were in danger of confiscation for in 1584 he conveyed his estates to trustees, leaving his nephew as a future life tenant only. But by 1589 Fitzherbert was paying £230 a year in recusancy fines, more than all his rents from Norbury, Padley, Hathersage or Hamstall Ridware.

Evidence suggests that while Sir Thomas was repeatedly restrained for contravening the Recusancy Acts, John Fitzherbert, his brother, ran his Padley estate and the mill, quietly living in Padley Hall where he and his wife reared 12 children. Padley was still the home of John Fitzherbert in 1588. Hathersage continued to ignore Anglican services at the parish church but there is no record that villagers were fined, although Vicar Haxall brought a case before the Bishop's Court in Lichfield against a Catholic, Thomas Barley, in 1590 for non-payment of church dues. A large bundle of case papers still exists which include the valuation of Barley's business with millstones and quarries.

Meanwhile George Talbot, 6th Earl of Shrewsbury, who among his many titles was lord of the manor of Hathersage by virtue of being Baron Crich, had now become Lord Lieutenant of Derbyshire. Eleven years younger than Sir Thomas and knighted at the same time, Shrewsbury's career had taken a very different turn. In the year that he married the wealthy widow, Bess of Hardwick, he was appointed custodian of Mary Queen of Scots, a duty he undertook from 1568 to 1584. He was an odd choice since his father had led a Catholic party when he was Lord President of the Council of the North from 1550-60 and the policy of confining Mary in lavish style in various houses in Sheffield and Derbyshire so close to a strongly Catholic area was a strange one. But while Mary was in his custody the Earl of Shrewsbury seems to have adopted a policy toward recusants of 'letting sleeping dogs lie'. In January 1588, however, the Privy Council ordered him to execute the requirements of the 1587 Act. On 29 January 1588 he targeted known recusants, delegating the task of searching to his Deputy, John Manners of Haddon Hall, who then gave the job to a local magistrate, Roger Columbell. Early on the morning of 2 February he and a band of men searched Padley Hall in vain. There were no priests in hiding. John Fitzherbert was away so Columbell took one of his sons into custody as well as a visitor, a remote relation and fellow Catholic, Richard Fenton of North Lees.

Shrewsbury took no further action except to complete over six weeks a short list of possible recusants posing a threat and needing to be put under surveillance. One was the aforementioned Richard Fenton, who was to be lodged with a suitable host at his own expense. Another was John Fitzherbert, who would be lodged with a preacher in Derby. Three and a half months went by and in early July 1588 John Fitzherbert was still at liberty at Padley. His brother, Sir Thomas Fitzherbert, now 71 years old, was in a London prison but able to supervise the collection of his rents and write letters.

Foreign affairs, however, were to determine the fate of John Fitzherbert. The Spanish Armada had set sail in earnest from Lisbon. The Queen and her advisors prepared to resist invasion by a Catholic power and Shrewsbury was aware that the prevailing mood in the Privy Council would not let him prevaricate any longer. He set about the unfinished task of tackling the recusant John

GEORGIVS TALBOTVS
COMES SALOPIÆ
AN·ÆTATIS 55
S·H
1580

36 *The 6th Earl of Shrewsbury d. 1590. As Baron Crich he was a chief lord of the manor.*

Fitzherbert, hoping to find him in defiance of the law. In the raid on Padley conducted by himself and his men on 12 July 1588 he found John Fitzherbert with some of his family and two priests. The famous story of the trial and martyrdom of Fathers Ludlam and Garlick belongs elsewhere. As master of Padley Hall, however, John Fitzherbert was liable to suffer the death penalty and confiscation of his property because he had harboured priests. It is possible that Roger Eyre, a son-in-law, bribed those in high places to avoid such penalties but this misfired and John was imprisoned in Derby county gaol for two and a half years and then transferred to a London prison in August 1590.

After John's arrest, Sir Thomas faced the loss of Padley and wrote on 28 May 1589 from prison to the Earl of Shrewsbury, his chief lord.

> I have found your honours [three generations of Shrewsbury] all my good lords, till now of late your Lordship's entering into the house of Padley found two seminaries there … since which time Your Lordship also hath entered upon the house of Padley and the demesnes thereof, seized all the goods of my brother's and mine that was in the house, amongst which I have certain evidences of a wood and meadow under Levin House called Faultcliffe [near Padley], which, as I am informed, your honour hath entered upon and occupieth wholly to your use, though I have been possessed and my wife's ancestors thereof time out of mind.

Seven months later, in December 1589, the Privy Council, mindful of the income from fines, ordered the Earl of Shrewsbury to hand over the property to tenants selected by Sir Thomas Fitzherbert.

In his new prison in London John Fitzherbert fell ill. Already in his sixties, three years of captivity had been enough to undermine his health and he died there three months later on 9 November 1590. On 10 January 1591 Sir Thomas was imprisoned in the Tower, where he died on 2 October 1591. He was buried in the Chapel Royal of St Peter ad Vincula in the Tower on 7 October. The Tower archives still have his records. It is a curious coincidence that two of Hathersage's lords of the manor were buried less than three miles apart in the East End of London in very different circumstances, Sir William Holles in St Helen's Church, Bishopsgate and Sir Thomas Fitzherbert in the Tower.

Chapter 14

Thomas Fitzherbert, Esquire

Thomas Fitzherbert, nephew of Sir Thomas Fitzherbert, on the death of his father, John, and uncle, was heir to the Fitzherbert estates and manors of Norbury, Hamstall Ridware and Hathersage. A practising Catholic when he married Elizabeth Westby, he had been named as heir by 1574 but by 1584 had become Protestant. As a result Sir Thomas, his uncle, changed the future arrangements for his estates. After the death of Sir Thomas and John, his father, Thomas Fitzherbert would only be a life tenant under trustees with no power to alienate the estate in any way.

Thomas Fitzherbert seems to have attended Queen Elizabeth's court; he certainly obtained the patronage of Robert Leicester until his death after the defeat of the Spanish Armada, and later fell under the influence of Richard Topcliffe, both a courtier and an agent of the Queen. After the death of Sir Thomas in the Tower in 1591, it was Topcliffe who persuaded the Queen to overrule Sir Thomas's will and to restore all the extensive estates of the Fitzherberts to Sir Thomas's nephew. Topcliffe himself then claimed the lease of the Padley estate as a reward. He occupied it and stayed ten years while Thomas, other Fitzherbert cousins and the Earl of Shrewsbury disputed ownership of the property in the courts.

Richard Topcliffe, Fitzherbert's unwanted tenant at Padley, was a Puritan extremist. Reputed to be well-born and educated, he was a Member of the 1586-7 Parliament expressing condemnation of Catholics in the wildest terms. In a speech of 24 February 1587 Topcliffe proclaimed the existence of Catholic plots, firing the House into a frenzy of fearful activity, which hastily created a committee of Puritan Members with quite illegal powers to search houses in Westminster for Catholic conspiracy. Topcliffe's denunciation found echoes in the Gunpowder Plot only 18 years later.

As well as being a spy for Queen Elizabeth, to whom he is reputed to have shown a bluff and vigorous loyalty, Topcliffe became a spy of the Privy Council, which charged him to hunt down and torture Jesuits and Catholic priests. Two of his most famous victims were a Jesuit missioner, Robert Southwell, and Father Pormort. It was a strange age when torture was condoned but judicial niceties were observed toward the victim. Topcliffe's methods and zealotry were to become too extreme for his masters and his royal employment ceased.

His love of Padley as a 'delightful solitary place' is out of keeping with the behaviour of this strange, sadistic man, in his sixties by 1600. His real intentions for Padley may have been spotted and curtailed by Thomas Fitzherbert, who forced the closure of the mill by a Privy Council warrant preventing lead smelting at Padley Mill. His argument was that the estate would lose value if the woodland were cut for fuel for the furnace. Topcliffe died in 1604 and his connection with Padley passed unmourned.

As for Thomas Fitzherbert, owner and lord of Hathersage and Padley, though not without challenge, it is ironic that his name should be of lasting importance in the constitutional history of the House of Commons. The House had already begun its

37 *Trees decimated for use as fuel for smelting furnaces.*

fight for independence from the Crown by claiming privileges of free speech, unrestricted elections and freedom from arrest for Members, and was close to ensuring that an elected Member must be safe from arrest and able to represent his constituency. In February 1593, however, Thomas Fitzherbert was elected as a burgess Member of the House of Commons for Newcastle-under-Lyme in Staffordshire. Two hours later he was arrested by the sheriff, who had not received the actual return paper. The charge related to the Queen's suit for debt and attracted 'outlawry', disqualification from being a Member of Parliament rather than loss of the protection of the law. The debt was £1,400 to the Queen and £4,000 to others. The suit was clearly an attempt on the part of the Queen to block Fitzherbert's election, and also indicated her concern that he was trying to avoid arrest by becoming an M.P., like some other candidates for elections. If that was Fitzherbert's motive for standing as a candidate (and he was the subject of 22 court cases for debt), he had not bargained for the Earl of Essex, the Queen's young favourite. Essex, also with an estate in Staffordshire, regarded the shire as his zone of influence and in February 1593 he filled eight out of ten possible parliamentary seats. Thomas Fitzherbert was not one of his choices and Essex may well have influenced the Queen's action against him.

Fitzherbert's arrest was the subject of a Report by a House of Commons Committee of Privileges in which opinion was divided. Fitzherbert was still in Staffordshire in the custody of his cousin and enemy, William Bassett, the sheriff. Long discussions began concerning the privilege of Members of Parliament to judge the validity of parliamentary elections, and these were to last the whole of the short Parliament. The Speaker, Sir Edward Coke, an intellectual giant even more famous in the next reign, battered the House with the depth of his legal knowledge.

Fitzherbert's arrest continued to be a *cause célèbre*. On 17 March William Bassett and Richard Topcliffe appeared at the Bar of the House to give evidence. Topcliffe used all his old alarmist powers to promote Fitzherbert's cause, doing more harm than good until the Speaker ordered him to be quiet. On 3 April the House had a record of Fitzherbert's debts. A Writ of Habeas Corpus from Chancery had been obtained for his release but not used for fear of offending the Queen. Then came news that Fitzherbert, in the custody of Sheriff Bassett, had arrived in London, and he was brought before the House to plead his case. On 5 April 1593 the Commons decided that although Fitzherbert was a Member he could not have privilege of freedom from arrest because the return had not been received by the sheriff, he was outlawed on a suit of the Queen and, finally, he had not been travelling to or from his seat in the House as a sitting Member.

The Commons were careful to the point of cowardice but, seeing the Queen's interest in the matter, their caution was understandable. The issue of freedom from arrest would reappear in Shirley's Case in 1604, early in James I's reign. Thomas Fitzherbert was an elusive figure in some ways, and little seen by Hathersage during the long legal challenges over his estates. He died in 1614 almost certainly in the Fleet Prison, London, a third lord of the manor of Hathersage to lie buried in east London.

Chapter 15

Transition to the Modern Age

There is a well-known contemporary description of Hathersage in 1587: 'There is some farms that be pritie yoman's livinge and a good sort of pritie farmes that keepe foure oxen apiece, besides the demaines of Padley and cotages.' This gives no indication of the tensions and undercurrents in the parish and manor of Hathersage at that time. In legal transfers of property, the ever-present phrase, 'saving the rights of the Chief Lord', came increasingly to refer to tenants paying rents rather than feudal dues, although the lord retained advowson in some churches, exercise of the court baron and control of mines and quarries.

The 7th Earl of Shrewsbury used the opportunity created by the inheritance struggles of the Fitzherbert family in the 1590s to take possession of the manor of Hathersage and Padley estate by 1601, thus drawing back to himself the lesser lordship. In spite of the challenge to his ownership, Shrewsbury rebuilt the disused Padley Mill in 1605, giving it a new chimney and bellows at a cost of ten pounds. Passing through many hands it continued as a smelting mill, and in the 18th century became a corn mill while the Hall itself fell into ruin. The other Fitzherbert nephews, heirs by Sir Thomas's arrangements at the time of his death in 1591, continued to contest ownership of the Fitzherbert estates including Hathersage and Padley Hall for the next fifty years. Although the wishes of Sir Thomas ultimately prevailed in a judgement of 1652, the Swynnerton branch of the family, to whom the Fitzherbert inheritance had passed, decided to sell the Hathersage lands and lordship in the 1650s in order to pay compensation and legal costs.

In Hathersage, as in Hope and Eyam, a new gentry was emerging in the late 16th century. Lead working operations, once small enterprises, now required more investment of capital to expand production. It was expensive to instal the pumps needed to penetrate deeper in mines and to introduce new processes in washing and smelting. The 'barons' of the lead industry and trade became the new gentry. They were rough mannered and treacherous, ignoring feudal niceties; not averse to risk, they were quick to gain an advantage over a competitor and unprincipled in taking over land or ideas patented by others. Evidence suggests that some of the Eyres, now of Highlow and Hassop, were no better: in 1625, the year of Charles I's accession, Robert Eyre of Hassop sought and obtained a general pardon for past felonies from the king. The disorder and unruliness were eventually curbed by the strict regulations of bodies like guilds and the lead liberties. Descendants of the original Padley Eyres sent their sons to Oxford and Cambridge and then to the Inns of Court to obtain some skill in the law. Robert Eyre, gentleman, was in Gray's Inn in 1564 and Edward Eyre was at the Middle Temple in 1592.

There were many other absentee landowners in Hathersage, while residents like the remaining Eyres had large holdings and industrial interests elsewhere. The Skinners, too, were wealthy landholders as were the Wickersleys, while the Vernons of Baslow had land in Offerton, Derwent and in Hathersage. The recusant Thomas Barley had investments in quarries and millstone production noted in the Tithe Case before the Bishop in 1590.

The names of tenants and recusants in 16th-century documents recur through their descendants in the church registers of the 17th century.

Feudal fealty had given way to a more useful attachment to a court faction or a great patron and manorial lordship commanded less esteem; it was sometimes divided and not infrequently sold, although more respect remained for the greater 'Lord of the Field'. While the lord's jurisdiction over villagers was almost extinct in Elizabeth's reign, his manorial court still controlled copyhold, husbandry and the management of common waste and moorland. The Hathersage records after 1656 show repeated prohibitions with increasing fines, suggesting that the manorial court was being ignored. Local power rested in the hands of Justices of the Peace, who were responsible for maintaining order, reporting recusants, and collecting a Poor Rate even before the Poor Law of 1601. The increasing prestige of

38 *North Lees Hall has Tudor origins.*

High Sheriffs and Lord Lieutenants provided royal supervision and national security.

After 1539 the parish church in Hathersage, like all other churches, was obliged to keep records and administer charities and poor relief, with the Churchwardens, Parish Clerk and Constable working to this end. Bess of Hardwick bought the parsonage and tithes in 1599 and her descendant, the later Earl of Devonshire, bought the patronage and presentation to Hathersage parish church in 1602 and appointed Edmund Harrop as vicar.

While many owners of properties and farms in Hathersage lived elsewhere, the increase in pasture farming in the Tudor period led to the appearance of the remote tenanted farmhouses with their enclosures on the hillsides and along the valley. Even today their 17th-century stone buildings remain, reminiscent of the Great Rebuilding of the Elizabethan Age.

The first years of James I marked a new age and the end of medieval attitudes. After the passing of Arthur Eyre, the mantle of Eyre ambition fell on the Eyres of Highlow, outside the parish and manor in the 17th century but still patrons of the church in Hathersage where they left their memorials. As for Hathersage itself, the focus of attention would move away from the old 'Padley within Hathersage' to the activities of local quarries, corn mill, smelting mills, bole furnaces, the malt house, the dwellings along the Dale, and the church on the hill.

Chapter 16

People of the Parish

From the Tudor period onwards we know the names of more of the four hundred people living in Hathersage and in the hamlets of the parish. In 1585, when precautions were being taken against Spanish attack, the names were listed of four men to be provided by Hathersage under the authority of John Manners and Robert Eyre, esquires. They were to join a muster at Bakewell with two callivers (firearms), one corselet of armour and one bill (halberd) between them. In 1587 four other men were to join a muster by May 1588 to be ready for action against the Armada if it landed. Other names are mentioned in the 1599 Subsidy List of the Hundred of the High Peak, when five people in Hathersage were sufficiently wealthy to pay a subsidy to the Queen, namely, William Jessop, gentleman, Richard Skynner, Thomas Eyre of Greenfoot, Nicholas Yellot and Thomas Eyre of Dingbank.

Even after the failure of the Armada, Queen Elizabeth's councillors feared the progress of Spain in its war against France and the doubtful loyalty of English Catholics. By 1593 the great spymaster, Sir Francis Walsingham, was dead so it was William, Lord Cecil, who prepared the Recusancy Lists of 1592-3 in addition to the earlier lists of known Catholics like the Fitzherberts of Padley and Fenton at North Lees. Thomas Barlow or Barley of Hurst appeared with his wife, as did Humphrey Padley, Robert and Alice Siddall, John Hawsworth, Thomas Slack and Miles Wilkin.

The monasteries had been the custodians of church records but when they were closed by Henry VIII the records were soon lost, so the king in 1539 required parish clergy to keep a record of christenings, weddings and burials. Even so, the records written on separate pieces of parchment or paper were often mislaid and an Act of 1597 therefore ordered that a parchment book be kept, to include the old entries going back to the 1530s, with each page being signed by the vicar and two churchwardens. This proved an impossible task in many parishes and in Hathersage surviving entries in the parish register begin, with the arrival of a new vicar, Robert Clarke, in March 1628 (New Style).

Written in Latin, the records of baptisms, marriages and burials were listed in chronological order until 1631 when they began to appear in separate sections. In the eight years from 1645-53 there were 20 baptisms of infants whose parents resided in areas other than Hathersage. This not only reflected the custom of young wives to return to their mother for the birth of their babies, but also demonstrated a preference for Hathersage's long-established Anglican priest, who was prepared to keep to the old ways in defiance of the new ordinances imposed by the Cromwellian regime.

In the archives of Chatsworth House there is a document written in 1618 listing Hathersage and Padley tithe payers, although no women's names appear. The tithe-paying householders or farm holders paid a tithe on corn. C has been added to note Catholics, based on Cecil's list or the parish register:

Barlow Thomas—C
Barker Andrew and Robert
Bayes Thomas
Brittlebank Thomas—C
Brownhiles Henry
Cam Hugh and Robert
Cotton John
Cowper Robert
Dakin Thomas
Dowe Anthony
Eyre Edward and Thomas
Farhourst Francis and Anthony
Fidler John—C
Foolow Francis

Frith Anthony
Greene Raffe and John
Hall Thomas
Held Anthony and John
Heton Thomas—C
Hodgkinson Thomas—C
Morton Thomas
Sile (Seele) John and William
Skinner Thomas—C
Smilter Lyon—C
Sylvester James
Tomasson Robert
Wilcockson, Francis
Wilcockson, John and Miles

Farmers paying only in wool and lamb

Coteril's farm
George Eyre's farm
Hiberson's farm
Thomas Hoyle's farm
William Hoyle's farm

Peter Morton's farm
George Morton's farm
Thomas Morton's farm
Tomasson's farm
Walker's house

Eyre was a common name and the numerous references to Thomas, William and Robert makes it difficult to decide which Eyre they mean. The entries sometimes help by mentioning where they lived as well.

To the north of Hathersage was an area occupied by the Catholic families of Skinner, Barley (Barlow) and Fox that appeared in a rental of 1638. There were a few farms and estates that had been rebuilt many times. These included Nether and Upper Hurst, Thorp, Burley and Gatehouse that may have constituted the berewick of 'Hirst' mentioned in Domesday Book, being the name transferred to properties of Hurst later. By the 17th century the area was called Hathersage Outseats, originally Ouset or Outstead, meaning a cluster of cottages or farms. In the early Hearth Tax lists of 1662-4, constables collected the Outseats tax separately from Hathersage until 1670, when the area was included in the Hathersage list, as were Bamford and Derwent.

In the parish register from 1628-55 there are entries for 82 burials by night (*noctu*), a practice by which Catholic families can be identified, although it is also clear that some branches of these families now conformed to the Anglican Church. By the 1650s reference to burials *noctu* was not being made and after the Restoration the term was seldom used in the register. A list of 11 tenants of the Fitzherberts in Hathersage and Padley in 1638 provides more names, including familiar Catholic ones: John Butler, Widow Cam of Moorseats, Widow of John Greene, Thomas Heaton, the Hodgkinsons, John Jacson (sic), Anthony and Francis Siddall, Francis Wilkin and Richard Sylvester of Padley. Protestant tenants included Robert Ashton and the Hathersage Dakins.

So the names of Hathersage families emerge from time to time, especially in the most complete Hearth Tax of 1670 and recusancy lists of 1705 and 1706. It would be some time yet before the Census of 1801 began the process whereby we can find our ancestors with more certainty.

Chapter 17

The Governance of the Parish

The parish church was the most important aspect of people's daily life: all must attend services on pain of fines; tithes or tenths of produce and work were to be paid to the vicar and churchwardens and it was the vicar and churchwardens who imposed law and order and laid down the rule of daily life, although Justices of the Peace of the counties, with parish constables, were responsible for punishment of crime as part of their duties. By the 17th century the court baron of the lord of the manor was mainly concerned with land transfer, leases and copyhold while his court leet kept watch on manorial custom.

When Edmund Harrop the vicar arrived in Hathersage in 1602 in the last year of Elizabeth I's reign his first task was to oversee the implementation of the Poor Laws of 1597 and 1601 and collect the Poor Rate from inhabitants of each parish to fund almshouses, pauper apprenticeships and houses of correction. The concept would not have been entirely new to Harrop and his churchwardens, for in some parishes these arrangements had been evolving already. Houses of correction, numerous in towns, were more scattered in the counties where more severe punishment was the alternative. The expense of such a house was too great for law-abiding parishioners, never far themselves from possible sudden disaster that could also take them to the brink of poverty. More often the culprits of drunkenness, riot and violence were brought to the assizes and county gaol. Hanging was the most common penalty for stealing a cow, sheep or horse. Poverty and crime were close companions.

Charities were also set up by devout people leaving legacies to establish almshouses, fund poor scholars, or provide donations of food or clothing on named church festivals within specified areas of the parish. The earliest known charity in Hathersage was endowed by Joan Morton. In her will of 1611 a portion of her estate provided funds for an almshouse which the recent Poor Laws had required each parish to have. Thomas Eyre of Crookhill, the executor of her will, died before he had obeyed her wishes. Three generations of his descendants ignored the terms of her will and that of Thomas Eyre, who also left legacies for the use of the poor. Finally, after a number of lawsuits by villagers against the descendants, a foundation deed was produced in 1642 based on an agreed settlement of £200 from Joan's house and lands at Aston in Hope parish. It stated that there should be six named governors to administer 'a hospital or abiding place for the poor to have continuance forever'. The poor were to be selected equally from each side of Chilbage Brook (now called Ladybower Brook), the intention being to help the poor of Derwent, Bamford, Outseats and Hathersage. There is no evidence that such a hospital or almshouse ever existed and the will may have referred to the Act of 1597 to ensure the charity's permanence. Since the flooding of the Derwent Valley for the 20th-century dams and the removal of local people, the Chilbage division has become irrelevant. The will has continued to be respected and to use the original capital and rents of Joan Morton's property. The moneys have been invested according to the financial plans available, in later periods using Pitt's Consolidated Funds of the 1780s or lending at interest to turnpike trust road schemes or War Bonds. Its original wording has been interpreted in a wide sense, which has enabled the Charity Commission to grant changes of interpretation to suit changing times. It is still in existence today under the careful control of governors and trustees. It is ironic that after such an inauspicious beginning, the Charity should have lasted so long.

The Hugh Barber Charity was based on his will of 1606 which after the death of the named heirs would pass to the churchwardens of Hathersage and Derwent to be equally distributed to the needy above and below Chilbage Brook. The capital came from land at Maltby and the rent of 22 shillings was payable on 1 March annually. In the 1827 report of the Charity Commission it was distributed with the Joan Morton Charity and was still in operation in 1856.

The key officers in the parish were the two churchwardens, who were appointed for a year at a time. They rarely stayed in office longer for theirs was a time-consuming task. Among their many duties they were responsible for the grants made to the poor from the poor rate, although overseers of the poor dealt with the practicalities.

Their other tasks are revealed in the annual accounts presented to the Hathersage parish meeting. Apart from paying the costs of a Bishop's Visitation, they paid from church dues for repair of the church fabric, including whitening the walls of the interior where Catholic images and altars had rested before they were torn down in the Tudor religious changes. They charged for the wood to burn the offending images. A new Communion Table and a desk for the Bible had to be paid for as well as the regular need of communion wine. At the parish meeting vacant pews and 'kneelings' or seats were reallocated according to property.

Collection and record of tithes was the most serious part of their work. The tithes of Hathersage parish church had been paid to Launde Abbey until the Lichfield diocese took over the appointment of the priest after a decision of the Royal Commission of 1395. Some dues for Launde remained until the Dissolution. The clergy themselves were poor. In 1585, in half of 9,000 livings, the income was reckoned to be no more than £10 a year. Many tithes were commutable and a sum of money would often make its way to the Dean and Chapter of the Cathedral. Perishable commodities like fish and meat had to be rendered in cash or sold to produce the tithe. Sending tithes in kind to a distant impropriator in order to return the parson's allocation for his income was not feasible. It is more likely that a reckoning was made and certain tithes were allocated to the vicar for his use, whether money or goods. In addition, Easter dues to the vicar appear in the churchwardens' accounts. Even beehives were counted, as were 'smokes' or fireplaces, a forerunner of the Hearth Tax of the 1660s. The vicar received other income including the Mortuary Fees for a funeral. The highest charge was for a burial with a coffin in the church itself. It cost less to be buried in the churchyard and even less to be buried without a coffin, in a shroud which had to be made of wool.

The parish clerk also listed his expenses and was paid fees for attending funerals and recording Catholic night burials, although the churchwardens made the official entry. The clerk had a seat below the pulpit in church from where he was expected to lead the singing of psalms and carols and announce the banns of marriage, and he often taught children their letters and how to count. This was a post that could last for years and ran in families like the Friths.

In spite of the watch kept by the villagers on each other from the cradle to the grave, parishioners were sometimes guilty of 'pagan' lapses. One such time would be All Hallows Eve, the time of prayers for the dead. It could result in unseemly behaviour, with the sound of horns and pipes, banging on surfaces and other disturbance. Superstition and fear of witchcraft also lurked just beneath the surface in the first half of the 17th century but the apparent reserve in Hathersage was safest in a period of religious extremes.

Chapter 18

The Highlow Eyres in the Stuart Period

Highlow Hall does not lie in Hathersage parish but the Eyres who lived there in the 17th century were involved with the village and warrant inclusion in our story as local entrepreneurs in mining and smelting lead. Descended from Robert Eyre I of Padley, the Eyres continued in three main lines to live at Highlow, Hassop and Holme Hall near Brampton. In the mid-15th century Highlow was occupied by John de Stafford of Highlow, the family of Stafford forging more than one marriage with the Eyres of Holme Hall. By 1570 Christopher Eyre, a grandson of Robert Eyre I of Padley, held Highlow Hall.

His descendants had dealings with lead smelting mills on the River Derwent and the family maintained ties with both Hope and Hathersage churches. In 1595 Robert Eyre, gentleman, was master of Highlow, with his wife Bridget, daughter of Sir Humphrey Ferrars of Tamworth. Two family deaths close together left Robert Eyre, a wealthy minor born in 1618, vulnerable to guardians seeking a young boy with property as a ward. An inventory dated 12 December 1633 describes his inheritance: the house at Highlow with its furniture, chattels, barns and mills and at least one lead smelt house. After his father's death in 1633 Robert was at first made a ward of the Crown until his wardship was sold to a John Dormer who, during the boy's minority, kept £400 a year and an interest in the lead mill. Selling a wardship like this was a typical way in which Charles I sought to raise money during his attempt to avoid calling Parliament in the so-called Eleven Years Tyranny of 1628-39.

As men of property, the Highlow Eyres were often involved in legal disputes. In 1615 Robert's grandfather was involved in a case in which Sir John Gell and Sir Francis

39 *Highlow Hall, home of 17th-century descendants of Robert Eyre.*

THE EYRES OF HIGHLOW HALL

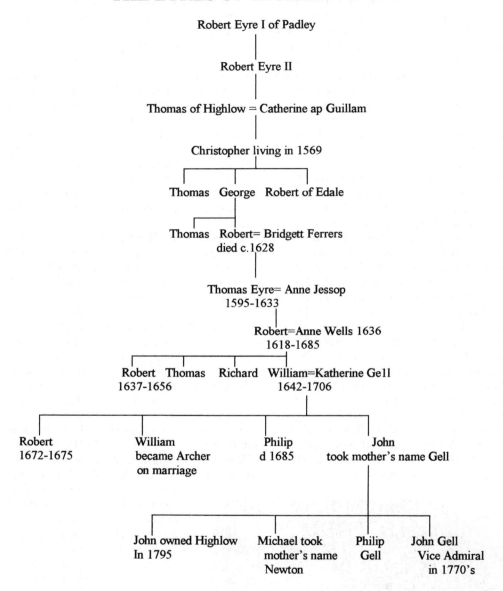

Robert Eyre I of Padley

Robert Eyre II

Thomas of Highlow = Catherine ap Guillam

Christopher living in 1569

Thomas   George   Robert of Edale

Thomas   Robert= Bridgett Ferrers
died c.1628

Thomas Eyre= Anne Jessop
1595-1633

Robert=Anne Wells 1636
1618-1685

Robert   Thomas   Richard   William=Katherine Gell
1637-1656   1642-1706

Robert   William   Philip   John
1672-1675   became Archer   d 1685   took mother's name Gell
                    on marriage

John owned Highlow   Michael took   Philip   John Gell
In 1795   mother's name   Gell   Vice Admiral
                      Newton   in 1770's

Leek at Bakewell sought to preserve their right to take a tenth of lead ore extracted from all mines in their lead liberties. Robert himself was the defendant in 1639 when he was taken to court for blocking a right of way between Highlow and Tideswell close to his leadmill near Highlow. He had planted a hedge across the old lane, which he ploughed up and incorporated in the next field while placing a gate in the hedge for access to the smelt mill. His neighbours confronted him and in the ensuing brawl he assaulted one John Eyre.

About 1636 young Robert Eyre married Anne, daughter of Bernard Wells, a wealthy lead merchant of Holme Hall near Bakewell, and they had four sons born just before the Civil Wars. Robert Eyre himself became more sedate and the earlier Eyre patronage of Hathersage church was continued with the gift of at least two of the bells in 1651 and 1659 which bear his initials and the same founder's mark. His public stance during the events of the Civil Wars gave a certain stability to the area. He became one of the Parliamentary gentry and was appointed to the County Committee in Derbyshire in 1644. In 1648 he became a Justice of the Peace and later joined a Committee to Eject Scandalous Ministers, usually Anglican clergy who did not conform to the new practices of the Commonwealth. Towards the end of the Cromwellian period he became High Sheriff of Derbyshire in 1657. After the Restoration of the Monarchy in 1660 Charles II commissioned a report to assess the 'Gentlemen of Derbyshire and how they stand affected'. It was noted that Robert Eyre had been a Colonel for the Parliamentarians and a Presbyterian (a conservative Puritan), 'but now I think, a convert'. Like many others Eyre practised a policy of accommodation with the victors of the day. He also speculated in land forfeited by Royalists. Surprisingly, he was not required to make the King a 'loan', as were so many of his persuasion.

In 1658 Bernard Wells died and for a time Robert Eyre lived in his father-in-law's Holme Hall in Bakewell. By now he held much property across the region. By 1670 he was a feoffee of the Free School at Hope and living at Highlow again, where he had nine hearths according to the Hearth Tax returns of that year. At his death in 1685, aged 67 years, he chose to be buried in Hathersage parish church.

Robert Eyre and Anne Wells had four sons, Robert baptised 17 February 1637, Thomas, Richard and William, the youngest, who was born in 1642. The first three are all recorded as undergraduates in Cambridge in 1656 and all were registered in Gray's Inn, London on 19 June 1656. A week later Robert died in Trinity College, Cambridge aged twenty. A plaque to his memory appears on another Eyre brass memorial in Hathersage church. Thomas, his brother, is recorded as being an undergraduate at St John's College, Cambridge and as a barrister in 1657, and in 1659 his name is recorded at Merton College, Oxford where he was possibly studying to gain a doctorate. William was 18 when in 1660 he registered at St John's College, Cambridge, having attended Mr Ogden's School, Buxton. In 1664 he married Katherine Gell, daughter of Sir John Gell (1595-1671), a notable local Parliamentary commander in the Civil Wars who, denounced by a rival, had been given life imprisonment in 1650 only to be pardoned in 1653. In 1670 William and Katherine were living at Holme Hall, Bakewell, and in 1685 William inherited his father's estates. It appears that Thomas and Richard, his brothers, had no heirs and had died by 1685, although their names do not feature in the burial register of Hathersage church.

The Highlow Eyres had numerous lead workings and also smelting mills, and like other local gentry sometimes leased their businesses. Although a few traces are still visible it is not easy to relate them to mills referred to in documents. Consisting of only a

40 *Traces of a corn mill on the river above Highlow once approached by an old green route.*

stone hearth, flues and chimney, no bellowed smelt mill still stands. Highlow smelting mill was leased to Robert Greg and others until his death in 1645 and a few ruins survive close to Highlow Brook above Highlow. There are traces of another smelting mill on the site of the present *Plough Inn* in a small hamlet now called Leadmill just to the east of the River Derwent. Clinker or lead waste has been found under the much altered features of the car park and field, and part of the site of the mill is almost certainly under the present road near the confluence of Highlow Brook and the River Derwent. The necessary water culverts are now part of a fish farm complex and channels run under the road close to the inn. The present Leadmill House in the parish of Hathersage was originally a corn mill on an island formed by its sluice in the River Derwent. When William Eyre married Katherine Gell in 1664 reference was made to smelting mills in the marriage papers. The last reference to lead working in this area appears in an inventory of 1676 concerning Hazelford Milne.

Although living at Holme Hall in 1670, William Eyre continued to regard St Michael and All Angels, Hathersage as a family church. The church register records the burial of Robert, his first-born son, in 1675 and of Philip, another son, on 11 March 1685. A Sheriff for Derbyshire in 1691, William Eyre was himself buried at Hathersage on 9 August 1706. A surviving son, also called William, later took the surname Archer on his marriage, a name relating to estates on his wife's side, and their son, John Archer, still held Highlow in 1795 together with other land worth £2,000 per annum, while his brother, Michael Archer, took his mother's maiden name, Newton, in order to receive an inheritance of family property. William and Katherine's other son took the name Gell to inherit Gell estates in Hopton.

Just as the Highlow Eyres lost their identity in these name changes, so the Hassop Eyres also changed their name. Francis Eyre was created Earl of Newburgh in 1823, and his sons inherited the title. The younger son, Francis, helped with the refurbishment in 1851 of Hathersage parish church and its Eyre tombs, restoring them to the condition we see today. There are many other Eyres buried in the church or nearby, whose tombs and brasses no longer remain, and the position of existing brasses has been changed. Where now is the dark coloured stone slab that J. C. Cox saw in 1877 under the altar with this touching inscription?

> Hic iacet Rob. filius primogenitus Gulielmi et Katarina Eyre de Highlow agro Derbiensis puer egregia forma et indole, parentum amor et delicia. Vixit 3 annos mense uno decemque diebus. Placide Deo anima reddidit.

> Here lies Robert, first born son of William and Katharine Eyre of Highlow in the county of Derby, a boy beguiling in form and talent, the love and delight of his parents. He lived three years, one month and ten days. His soul returned gently to God. 3rd June 1675.

Although the reputation of the Eyres is obscured by legend, records of this long-lasting family of middle gentry speak of their attachment to Hathersage and surrounding areas. They were local lead employers and farming landowners as well as quarry masters. They made a lasting impact on the area by their industry, enterprise and patronage of the parish church.

Chapter 19

The Civil Wars and the Interregnum 1642-1660

As the Civil War gained momentum, Royalist and Parliamentary armies from Sheffield, Chesterfield and Bakewell skirted the Hope Valley, avoiding its possible trap and shadowing each other as they moved toward key areas. They swept up local men, who often followed the lead of local gentry into areas far from home, where they were sometimes disbanded. The campaigns were often of short duration with lulls in the fighting in winter.

People remaining in the village paid their taxes and kept silent. Already vicar for 18 years, Robert Clarke ran into difficulty, committed as he was to the old ways. As early as 1645 use of the Book of Common Prayer in church was prohibited. Instead the Directory, the guide to the new services, was to be used. After Cromwell's victory at the Battle of Preston in February 1648 a contingent of the defeated Royalist army continued to march to Uttoxeter, before the remaining troops finally broke up into bands and drifted home to Scotland. The soldiers were very vulnerable, living off the land and at the mercy of local people. In Chapel-en-le-Frith some 1,500 of them were shut up in a church for a fortnight. Over forty died before the survivors were driven out. A smaller band arrived in Hathersage and the parish register for 21 October 1648 records, 'One Scot and twenty three other Scots buried in Hathersage'. One can only guess at the events leading to this entry and the vicar's dilemma.

The Protectorate discouraged clergy from keeping parish registers. Following an ordinance of 1653 registration of christenings, marriages and deaths was to be made to a designated civilian at a cost of 4d. for each entry. Marriages were to be made before a Justice of the Peace in a civil ceremony, although vows were often made afterwards in secret if a sympathetic minister could be found. It tells us much about Vicar Clarke that he persevered so long with his records. After his death in July 1655 the parish had to wait 13 months for Clarke's successor, John Kelsall, who was installed as vicar on 11 September 1656, having been approved by the political regime. There is a break in the registers for he made no entries, in accordance with the orders of the regime that appointed him. The Easter Tithe List was still required for taxation purposes but the Hathersage lists of this date have not survived, although there is one of 1658 in neighbouring Hope. The Protectorate had by then realised the potential of this church fee, which they put to secular use. Parish registers were kept again after the Restoration in the time of the next vicar, John Walker, whose induction in late 1662 was recorded in the Bishop's Transcripts.

In this period of political change in the mid-17th century there were new developments in agriculture. The estates of Royalist nobility and gentry were often sequestered and their farms taken over, but if they regained their property it was not uncommon for them to apply new methods learned in exile abroad. Fen reclamation had been in progress since the 1620s in East Anglia, undertaken by a Dutchman, Cornelius Vermuyden, on the King's orders, but it was his Dutch colleague, Major John Molanus, who worked on problems of Derbyshire drainage for Sir John Gell, Robert Eyre's associate. It is generally thought that Molanus was responsible for the reclamation of the land on the banks of the River Derwent, at least between Nether Hall and the modern Leadmill, and that the names New Close and New Leys relate to this period in the 1650s.

There was a new understanding of the value of clover, not only as a grazing crop but also for its enrichment for soil and Hathersage and nearby villages record local clover fields by name in the 17th century. Pest control was important to arable farmers always at the mercy of predators and vermin. There are numerous records of rewards by the churchwardens for the heads of foxes, boursons (badgers) and orchins (hedgehogs).

Hathersage was associated with flax growing and processing for spinning in the mid-17th century, when linen and fustian production was at its height in England. Flaxlands was noted in 1655 as one of John Heald's fields, and Flaxyard was a property mentioned in a land purchase by Woodroffe. Flax dressing was a lengthy and delicate process for rendering stems into yarn ready for linen weaving. Flax *usitatissimum* was valued for the stems which were pulled right down to the root to obtain long fibrous strands. The stems were laid out to dry in the fields and then soaked for up to six weeks, a process called 'retting', to separate the fibres from the woody stalk. This process generated a foul smell. Dried again in the fields, stalk and seeds removed, the fibres were hackled with a comb to achieve the finest and longest threads.

Hemp, a very similar plant, was also processed locally in the 17th century in the Hempyard owned by John Morton. The Hempyard was in the vicinity of Dale Brook, which now runs through a culvert between the NatWest Bank and Post Office. Hemp was used not only for huckaback, sailcloth and sacking but also for ropes. As local lead mines went deeper in the 17th century such products were vital for hauling miners and loads, and it is very possible that John Morton's Hempyard met some of the local needs. The industry continued for a long time: as late as 1827 George Stones of Hathersage is described as apprentice to a flax dresser and rope maker.

As early as 1566 a German called Christopher Schultz is said to have established a wire-drawing operation in Hathersage. As well as meeting demand from local lead miners for ore sieve baskets necessary in the dressing stage, wire was needed to make hackle combs and wool-carding combs. Widely used in the village, Schultz's process was eventually stopped by a patent of Sir William Humphray, an Elizabethan courtier and the Assay Master of the Royal Mint. Wire-drawing thereafter became an occasional local occupation and hackle pins for the combs were manufactured commercially to serve local textile needs. These combs, consisting of different gauges of pin grouped on a wooden block to comb the tough hanks of flax, became a speciality in the future of at least one mill in Hathersage, which proclaimed in an 1851 catalogue that it was the only place where hackle pins were made.

Hathersage was closely involved with lead smelting and dressing and place-names and geographical features recall this old industry. Many 'bole hills' remain, although bole hearths sited in high windy places were obsolete by the 17th century and their simple structures soon disappeared, to be replaced by new ore hearths with bellows dependent on fuel from coppiced woodlands. The most important requirement for a smelting mill was proximity to the precious commodity of wood. Later bellowed mills were built near brooks and rivers to drive their water wheels. The gentry had once worked or leased their simple bole hearths but now newcomers with more capital were able to apply more expensive smelting processes. They in turn would create partnerships to introduce new technological changes until the cupola operation of the 18th century.

In 1652 the long-running Fitzherbert case regarding the family's property ended when Chancery ruled in favour of the Fitzherberts of Norbury. To meet the costs and compensation required by the judgement, preparations were made to sell all the Fitzherbert estates in Padley and Hathersage. The sales ran over three years from 1655-7 and brought many new landowners like the Ashtons to the village. The fragmentation of the Fitzherbert estate and the sale of the lordship necessitated a manorial perambulation that took place in 1656 to define the boundaries of the manor and parish of Hathersage. They were shown in a court baron paper of 1656 which also recorded the state of the manor and defined the copyhold conditions of tenure according to 'the Rolls of ancient custom'. The court baron proceeded with its usual work by setting dates for the winter opening of named gates for animals to graze on harvested crop fields and enrich the soil with manure. Dates were also set for the spring closing of gates and removal of beasts before the next ploughing and planting of crops and cereals. Peasant cultivators were granted varying quotas or 'gates' allowing a certain number of their beasts onto common land, and fines were laid down for people who let their fowl and beasts stray on the public road. There were also fines for selling peat and fern and for burning soil out of time, all old concerns of medieval court barons. These regulations and penalties would continue in the 18th-century court barons until the period of parliamentary enclosures.

Chapter 20

From Restoration to Revolution

Charles II was invited to come to the throne in 1660 after the breakdown of order in the last years of the Commonwealth, when even some judges had refused their commissions and the military broke into factions. Charles, returning from Holland and experienced in the misfortune of exile, was conciliatory, but his promise to those of tender conscience proved unworkable in the face of the prevailing attitudes of the Restoration Parliament. From 1661–5 Acts were passed to enforce Anglican uniformity, one requiring all clergy to use the Book of Common Prayer, leading to many Puritan ministers giving up their livings. This certainly happened in neighbouring Eyam and may have been the case in Hathersage for there was a change of vicar in late 1662.

An immediate issue for Parliament and the King was to agree changes in taxation. A Hearth Tax was devised, to be collected by constables and sheriffs half yearly at Lady Day and Michaelmas. The local collection lists of 1662 and 1664 give the names of householders and an insight into their status. It is not certain if Bamford and Derwent were included under Hathersage, although they were in the 1670 tax list, together with Outseats. The names of 130 householders with a hearth are listed, so a multiplier of five for an average family suggests a population of six hundred and fifty.

Parish rates were now inadequate to support the increasing number of poor. Parliament's solution was the Act of Settlement of the Poor of 1662. Its intention was to regulate the application for relief by travellers moving through parishes; its effect was to restrict travel. Justices of the Peace and parish constables were authorised to send any newcomer back to his last place of domicile if liable to become a charge on the parish. Over the years this was modified to allow a traveller to produce a certificate from his last parish acknowledging liability if he became destitute. Once in a new parish an incomer was entitled to claim settlement by renting a house worth over £10 a year. The new parish could accept his presence safe in the knowledge that he would not become a burden.

A later development was the passport, or 'letter of request', given to travellers as they set out on a journey and stating their place of origin and destination. There are numerous instances in Hathersage of the law in action. Simon Dakin, the constable in 1678–9, had 11 passports presented that year and the travellers received amounts in the region of 1s. 6d. or 2s. Their journeys were often long, from Oban to Plymouth or Southampton to Cumberland. It is remarkable that their routes took them through such desolate and wild country. The method of assessment varied according to the number travelling and their circumstances. By 1680 Outseats had become a civil parish insofar as it now dealt with its own certificates of settlement.

The Act of Settlement of the Poor must be borne in mind when considering what happened in Eyam after plague arrived in 1665. Plague was endemic in Sheffield and local instances in Derbyshire had occurred in 1646. In 1665 it broke out in London and a package from there seems to have brought the plague to Eyam, where many died. The popular story is that the villagers under the lead of the rector and the old Cromwellian minister chose to confine themselves within the limits of the village. In fact, a few gentry did leave in the early days but the villagers were trapped because of the Act of Settlement. People in other parishes, fearful at any time of yet another call on their poor rates, were terrified of the plague. One woman escaping from Eyam was turned back at Woodseats outside Sheffield, while another was driven away by a crowd at Tideswell. The pitiable folk of Eyam would have found no haven. The rector and minister need not have stayed but by remaining they gave the people their support and made a virtue of necessity. In the second year the plague returned after a lull with renewed ferocity. Only then did the two clergy seem to urge the villagers to continue their segregation. In the face of so many deaths, this was a very hard decision.

There is a story that the people of Eyam left coins in a spring called Mompesson's Well in return for food and supplies. This is unlikely because in the months of their seclusion the supply of coins would have been exhausted. Food and supplies were certainly left for the village by the Earl of Devonshire and others but as gifts to augment the villagers' dwindling stock and resources.

The isolation of Eyam served to prevent the plague reaching nearby villages like Hathersage. Although the burial register of Hathersage parish church is not complete from 1665-6, the records in the Bishop's Transcripts shown that deaths were within the usual annual mortality rates and make no mention of plague. The vicar of Hathersage, John Walker, is known to have met Rector Mompesson on Eyam Moor, writing a dictated letter for him though keeping a healthy distance. Eyam's rector is believed to have dictated births and deaths to Walker in this way, leaving an uncontaminated record should he too die of plague. The original records no longer exist but these sheets seem to have formed the basis of the Bishop's Transcripts after 1666. The thought of the two clergy in such circumstances, shouting to each other on the high slopes above Eyam, fires the imagination.

The parish constable had to maintain law and order and the range of his duties features in his accounts. He charged for attendance at petty sessions and for refreshment there for himself and jurors from the parish: for a journey to the Buxton Assizes, a day's ride, the charge was 2s. including refreshment. In one year there were three 'hue and cries' passing through the parish, which the constable joined. He took a thief for branding, took William Slynn to trial for stealing a sheep, and then to Wardlow Miers to be hanged for the offence, and charged 13s. 6d. He supervised the ducking of Mary Gates in the river with the ducking stool.

The Hathersage churchwardens assisted the vicar and had much authority; their remit was wide-ranging. The accounts include visitations from Lichfield Cathedral, when the dean, the bishop or an archdeacon had to be entertained and shown the current accounts of the glebe and church land. The vicar's surplice and altar linen must be washed, but infrequently. Sweeping the 'rubbige' from the church appeared regularly as did the purchase of bread and wine for communion and oil for lamps. Nails were bought constantly. Books had to be bought for special occasions from the Apparitor, the Dean's secretary: a treatise for 5 November, or a 'day of humiliation' in 1674, or a homily for 30 January in 1694, no doubt commemorating the execution of King Charles I in 1649.

Repairs in the church were never-ending: a plumber was to work on the leads of the windows and see to the glazing; lime and hair were bought to mix for plastering interior walls; the steeple was pointed with a mixture of mortar and beer. Repair of the altar happened more than once and stone was laid in the body of the church. A new feature in 1686 was a rail before the altar and soon a mat was provided on which to kneel at the rail. A bier was purchased and two communion plates.

The churchwardens kept constant watch on the state of the bells. By 1680 there were six, not counting the little 14th-century Sanctus Bell. Although they had been used since the Middle Ages to tell the village the time and call it to services, wheel mounting, introduced in the 17th century, produced a great change as bells could now be turned through a full circle. This in turn opened the way for change ringing, which developed after 1658. The six bells in Hathersage had new ropes and leathers nearly every year. The ringers were paid for special occasions such as the defeat of the Duke of Monmouth's army in 1685, or the accession of James II, or the Queen being with child and, later, her safe delivery. They rang for the new King and Queen, William III and Mary II, brought to the throne by the Glorious Revolution of 1688. The language of the bells distinguished between ordinary daily events and great news. In the 18th century they would ring for victories in Europe, America and at sea. They would celebrate Trafalgar when that news came in 1805.

A new level of organised charity was imposed on parishes in the 1680s. Letters patent or 'briefs' issued by the Privy Council required them to make contributions to funds for victims of calamity elsewhere, ranging from merchant hostages in Turkey to Irish Protestants for whom money was needed in 1689 and after Louis XIV had finally forced the expulsion of Huguenots from France in 1686. Many had already come to England and money was being collected for them. A letter patent was read out in church and churchwardens had to see to the collection of money round the parish for fire damage to buildings throughout England, be they sugar houses in London, sawmills in Surrey, a collapsed steeple in Oxford or others in Southwark, Bungay or Knaresborough. The churchwardens accounts are not available after 1693 but Hope's accounts continue until 1720 and the briefs would have been the same for Hathersage.

While briefs had the effect of widening the horizons of people in remote villages there was still room for private charity. Thomas White bequeathed his property in Hathersage to fund a charity for the Vicar (of Hathersage) and Poor of Stoney Middleton, a curacy of the parish. Six named trustees were to run it. Twenty-six brown loaves were given on St Thomas's Day near Christmas and a shilling's worth of meat twice a year. Other funds were available to the Overseers of the Poor. The charity is still in existence, although Stoney Middleton later became a parish in its own right.

Catholics were now seen as less of a threat. The later Stuart kings had married Catholic princesses and after the Restoration the religion was favoured at court. People became alarmed when Titus Oates in 1678-9 fanned the rumours of a Catholic conspiracy against the royal family. When James II, a Catholic, became king, he relaxed the recusancy laws illegally. His second wife, Mary of Modena, was Catholic and the last straw for his subjects made increasingly fearful by the king's illegal activities was the birth of a son to her, although in the village the bells were dutifully rung. They were rung too for the ensuing Glorious Revolution of 1688 which brought Protestant William and Mary to the throne.

In this unpromising period Adam Furniss made a deed granting land for a Catholic chapel in Hathersage which was built in 1692. A later note written by a Jane Hobson states that the Catholic chapel standing in Furniss Field was attacked and made unusable by a Protestant mob. It has been suggested that the attack was instigated by those involved in the invitation to William and Mary to take the throne but there is no evidence for this. The newly elevated Duke of Devonshire, who had been a party to the deliberations, would not have seen fit to disrupt Hathersage in the lordship of the Duke of Newcastle, his cousin. The chapel was not rebuilt until 1806, over a hundred years later.

Chapter 21

Hathersage in the New Era

As Britain slipped into a new century the pace of business life was revolutionised. The Bank of England in 1695 had transformed financial trading in the City of London, which in turn gave impetus to individual enterprise in industry and commerce. The East India Company's exclusive trade with the East and India expanded greatly and England benefited from the cargoes of cotton, tea and coffee brought by larger fleets of sailing ships arriving seasonally on the Trade Winds. These changes were to filter through Britain, altering the systems of local trade and manufacture.

41 Hill, the lost hamlet, had shops and houses in 1750s. Its last buildings are to the north. Its fields shown here are post enclosure on high ground called Ranmoor Hill.

In the Hope Valley church bells would be rung for the coronation of Queen Anne, the last Stuart ruler, and for George I the first Hanoverian, in 1714. England and Scotland had officially become the United Kingdom on 1 May 1707, and when the Jacobite Rising of 1715 failed it was due less to the Old Pretender's ineptitude than his intention to repudiate the National Debt. Investments like the South Sea Bubble were not without their victims, like Mr Gisbourne who was ruined by its collapse in 1720; it was mooted that he might have to sell his Bamford estate 'as he has been dipped in the South Sea stock'.

The Hearth Tax records of 1670 for Hathersage, including Derwent, part of Bamford, Booths, Outseats and Padley, list 131 properties, giving about 600 to 700 people. By 1767 Burdett's map showed rather indistinctly 76 properties, but he was selective in excluding very small houses. Thirteen farm hamlets including North Lees and Carr Head lay high on the hillsides. No house qualified for the description of 'hall' in the environs of Hathersage, not even at Offerton or Eyam, although their great houses existed. 'Halls' must wait until the pretensions of the 19th century.

The only church in Hathersage was still the parish church standing on its hillock with the small vicarage. Unlike many churches throughout England, it was not the beneficiary in architectural terms of the famous Queen Anne's Bounty, although the Bounty still augmented the stipend of the Hathersage incumbent in the 20th century. The little green below the church was edged with cottages and more, including a farm today known as the *Scotsman's Pack*, faced the brook along the Dale track that was to become a turnpike in 1758. Micchell Field Farm lay higher up the valley. Hathersage 'Hall', bought as a farm by the 1680s by Robert Ashton, the lead magnate of Stoney Middleton, became the residence of his descendants, the Spencers of Cannon Hall near Doncaster, and later the Shuttleworths. A group of cottages and houses were clustered close to what is now the narrowest part of the main street. Two or three farms stood further down the village street. The inn we know as *The George* was the place most used for the court barons of the 18th century, as it would be used later for enclosure meetings and inquests. There was a corn mill in the vicinity of the present Nether Hall. Mills tend to reinvent themselves, corn grinding giving way to lead dressing and cotton spinning in some areas in the Hope Valley later in the 1780s. Near Greens House, high above Hathersage, another mill was smelting lead in the 1720s and making paper in the 1760s. By the end of the century another enterprise was button making at Dale Mill on Dale Brook.

42 *All that remains of the village green by Hathersage church.*

In 1718 a school had been built on land given to the poor of Hathersage by Benjamin Ashton at Geer Green high up Coggers Lane. Thomas Eyre wrote that there was a public subscription and Ashton had given 10 guineas at the start to educate six poor boys. In 1719 he says, 'The Scollmaster [*sic*] boards with us and is a very civill good humoured man and a good scoller.' On his death in 1725 Benjamin Ashton's will gave the schoolmaster an extra £5 a year to teach ten of the poorest boys in Hathersage and Outseats, provided that Ashton's heirs had the nomination of future schoolmasters. The schoolroom with its two small side rooms was in disuse by 1807 and it no longer exists. Today the site seems lonely and impractical but it indicates the size of the local population in the hamlet then called Hill. A cottage near the Gatehouse road, rented in 1752 as a Poor House, was also mentioned in the enclosure papers. Nearby farms like Burley, Gatehouse, North Lees, Hurst and Upper Hurst, Thorpe and Greens House had labourers' cottages and plots nearby. There were five such units at Moorseats according to the

43 *A 17th-century cottage called Thimble Hall at the narrowest part of the main street.*

researches of James Holworthy in the 1820s. There were no children using Geer Green School when a new schoolroom was established by public subscription in 1804, to be situated in what is now the Parish Room where the subscribers are listed on a board. Henry Ibbotson, a major donor, gave an additional £82 to form a charity paying the schoolmaster to teach three poor children of Outseats from the interest. Mr Thomas Cocker borrowed the capital at five per cent on security of the Sheffield turnpike and supervised the payment.

There is no doubt that many older and insubstantial houses, cots, tofts and hovels have collapsed and disappeared. On the east side of the present A6187 below the Surprise View there are signs of primitive booths with their animal runs. Only sturdier houses survived and they were much adapted or encased in 18th-century facades. Over time two small cottages might be made into one home. The first consideration in building a new house was that it should have a water supply such as a spring or the site for a well to be dug. To be too near a river invited flooding. The name 'Nether Hall' appears in the land sales of the 1650s, when the messuage was bought by Thomas Eyre of Allport and leased to a tenant, Andrew Barker, whose family held the messuage and the reclaimed fields near the river into the 18th century. The name seems not to describe a building but to indicate a site by the confluence of two rivers 'nether (or below) Offerton Hall'. In 1713 the parish register records that James Hobson drowned in Lady Bower Brook

44 *A sketch of the 1758 turnpike at its lower end in the Dale in E. Rhodes' book* Excursions in Derbyshire.

45 *The subscription list for the new school of 1804, known as Marsden's School after the schoolmaster.*

46 *Hathersage in Burdett's Map of Derbyshire, 1791.*

in the October and was found in the River Derwent at a place known as Nether Hall. In 1787 a court baron had business with John Wilcockson, yeoman of Nether Hall, concerning all the messuages named the Marsh or Marle. John Shuttleworth bought the land in 1839 and the present Hall was built shortly after.

In the 1790s Hathersage's economy fell into decline. There were many more pauper deaths in the church register and by 1810 a dozen houses lay empty. The effects of war with France from 1793 may have contributed but the long-term effects of the industrial and agrarian revolutions of the 18th century played a greater part.

Kindly people provided money in their wills to support charities to help the poor. In 1720 Adam Morton left £10 for the interest to be given to the poor, especially widows, in Hathersage. Robert Crossland later augmented the sum with a donation of £6 13s. 4d., the capital being lent in 1805 to Mr Thomas Cocker at five per cent interest and administered with the Morton Charity. Richard Sylvester had left 1s. 3d. in 1760 with Seel Field behind the present school as security. In 1790 John Shuttleworth, the field's owner, was paying out the sum to the poor of Hathersage with Derwent receiving one shilling. John Frost in his will of 1773 gave 15s. to be divided between Hathersage, Outseats and Derwent and John Furniss, an heir, was still paying it in 1827. The Rev. Francis Gisborne left £5 10s. a

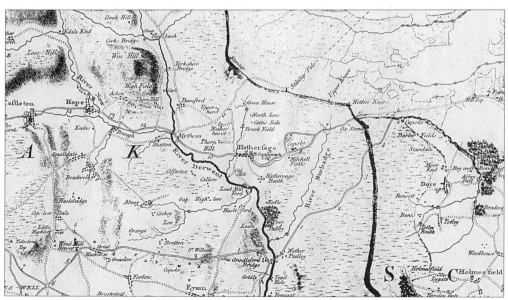

year separately to each hamlet to
provide wool and clothes to the
poor at Christmas.

No charity exists forever, in
spite of the expectation of some
donors. Robert Turie's Charity,
established in a will of 1720, left
money to educate six poor children
of the Derwent area, close to Abbey
and the property that funded the
charity. By 1807 the capital was
eroded after the bankruptcies of
its trustee, George Littlewood, and
of Hans Winthrop Mortimer of
Mortimer Road fame. Sometimes

47 *The floor of an earlier cottage found
under a drive on Church Bank in 1989.*

the capital was too small to survive or later conditions invalidated the original intention.
Charities often named St Thomas's Day for issuing the bounty and, where possible, in
more modern times the little charities with similar conditions have been administered
together with the Joan Morton Charity. The Charity Commission at Liverpool keeps
watch over them and gives its blessing when their terms can be reinterpreted to meet
modern needs within the spirit of the original donation.

The tracks, green lanes, holloways and coffin paths that linked remote hamlets within
Hathersage parish are barely visible today and are mostly long forgotten. In 1720 Thomas
Eyre wrote to Archer that there was a 'former private' way from Offerton Hall and, as for
the 'corpse path' from Highlow to Hathersage church, only two men could remember it.
Fords and stepping stones rather than bridges crossed the rivers. The packhorse route to
Sheffield bypassed Hathersage altogether, turning east at Hill Foot and giving its name to
today's Jaggers Lane. Another track led southward from the present *George Inn* to the old
mill near the river, and on to the Leadmill Ford, then past Hazelford to Leam and Eyam.
Another, called Booth Lane, led from Hathersage eastward up the hill to Hathersage Booths
where it stopped. The first turnpike road would only come in 1758, following the old
Dale track past the Cupola and nearby farms up to Overstones. It ran along the steep edge

of the Burbage Valley and turned
sharply onto the Burbage Bridge,
a difficult manoeuvre for coaches
which invited the attentions of
thieves. Some of the slopes were
very steep for horse-drawn wagons
and various types of wedge were
used to stop wheels rolling back
or hurtling forward. These were
called 'scatches' or 'scotching stones'
and would be supplied by nearby
dealers. One hamlet near Belper
took its name of Scotches from
the wedges. In Hathersage the
so-called *Scotsman's Pack Inn* may
be associated with an old scotch
collection point.

48 *The old stepping stones linking Offerton with the packhorse
route up Jaggers Lane. A ford is nearby.*

Chapter 22

Local Industry

Until the mid-18th century there were few public carriage roads in the Peak. Hathersage parish was notoriously difficult for travellers and routes were impassable in winter, although on one occasion in the bad winter of 1739-40 William Spencer of Hathersage Hall wrote that the tracks were 'so frozen as hard as iron that they were as good as in summer'. Although Justices had been responsible since 1555 for maintaining roads using the unpaid labour of parishioners, the vast and steep moors of Hathersage parish defeated them. With travel almost impossible in winter, millstones and lead were moved in summer towards the trade centres of Sheffield, Derby and Staffordshire and the river ports of Bawtry and Gainsborough. The Hassop Eyres, important lead merchants, had a house in Bawtry on the River Idle where freight was shipped to the Humber, and Rowland Morewood, a businessman and property owner of Hathersage in the 17th century, bought a wharf on the River Trent.

The Quarry Masters

One of the remarkable aspects of the beautiful Hope Valley in which Hathersage lies is the different appearance of the east and west hillsides. To the west of the River Derwent there are the rounded slopes of limestone, while to the east the edges of Millstone Grit rise sharply to dramatic heights. Burbage or Reeve Edge looms over Burbage Brook. Further west the view of Hope Valley opens up so suddenly where Booth Edge, or Millstone Edge, drops to Millstone Quarry on its west flank, it is called the Surprise View. Soaring above the village to the north-east is the impressive Stanage Edge, running towards Bamford Edge.

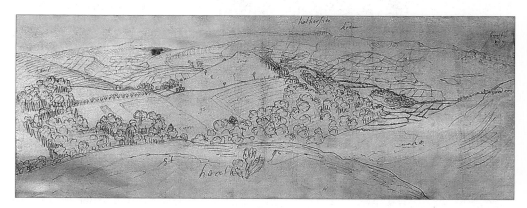

49 *A panoramic sketch for a proposed 18th-century hall near Hathersage.*

50 *Stanage Edge, where millstones were quarried.*

The Eyres and other families had been quarrying since the Middle Ages. Grindstones were cut for use in cutlery and iron finishing, while millstones were made in pairs to grind wheat and other cereals. Wills and inventories in the 17th century show that stone cutters owned not only their own tools but also the stones they had made on the moors and in quarries. Marks found on the stones were masons' marks, although later they indicated the quarry of origin or the buyer's order. Some stones would have the convex mushroom shape on one face, a common feature in the 17th century.

Independent millstone men could sell on to merchants but they could also become carriers or merchants themselves. Quarries nearer Sheffield provided stones for the metal trade but a living could be made by selling to agents and merchants of big ports like King's Lynn, Colchester and Southampton. Francis Dakin, probably the same tenant besieged for a time at Padley during the legal quarrels over the Fitzherbert estate, once supplied 42 pairs to agents visiting the Peak. When they were delivered to Bawtry, his representative, Thomas Dakin, received payment for them. Dakin lived on Fitzherbert land at

51 *Millstone quarry at the Surprise View.*

52 *Millstones abandoned close to where they were made.*

Hathersage Booths, as did Simon Dakin later. His millstones and tools were listed in the inventory of his property in 1663. This local family was one of many, like the Wilcocksons, Siddalls and Roddiards, engaged in stone-cutting.

By the 18th century these stonecutters had lost their independence. The lords of the manor or great landowners usually leased quarries to tenants. In 1684 John Rotherham of Dronfield, an important quarrymaster elsewhere, paid £80 a year to take a lease on all the Hathersage quarries owned by the Pegges, then technically lords of the manor. By 1722 Samuel Rotherham had leased Bamford Edge from Mr Gisbourne and also worked Millstone Edge, including nearby sites like Oller Tor. Such was the monopoly of the Rotherhams that they paid low wages and provided tools to their twenty or so workers, probably to prevent them working elsewhere; workers had become employees.

We gain a clear picture of how quarries were run from correspondence relating to an abortive attempt to cut millstones on the Offerton slopes of the Highlow estate. William Archer, the landowner of Highlow, was persuaded to enter the market. An Eyre by birth, he had changed his name on marrying the heiress of the Archer fortune. He lived in the south of England and for a time relied on a relation in Hathersage, Thomas Eyre of Thorp, to manage the family property. Thomas recommended the opening of Offerton quarry and, although semi-literate, his letters to Archer offer insights into the local quarry business. Workmen liked the 'mettle' of the stone and trials were made. It was found that the bottom stone was too 'fine' but the top stone promised to yield hundreds of pairs of millstones. The enterprise was begun by 1720 but within a year Eyre himself reported the stone at Highlow to be 'full too soft', although the site was worked for another couple of years.

The precarious and ruthless business of millstone working included poaching workmen from other employers. Eyre discovered that Rotherham's workers were bound not to make stones on leaving him by a £50 bond. Men were hired for a year at a time on piece rates, according to the size of the stones measured in 'hands'. None would move for the same wage so Archer was advised by Thomas Eyre to offer a higher one. Eyre also exploited a quarrel between Rotherham and his workmen in 1721 that had caused 15 of the 21 workers to leave him. Eyre employed three, including an old mason who advised him how to obtain the most millstones from a single rock. 'Cutting to the best husbandry is the greatest piece of ingenuity,' Eyre comments. He wanted to quarry with a friend on a sublease at Bamford Edge but under Archer's name, so 'Mr Rotherham will not hector over us and stop them taking away the stones'. The scheme did not happen.

Transport of stones was difficult and expensive. The usual route to Bawtry, 'for going on water' beyond Sheffield, was on the east side of the River Derwent, but the weakness of bridges and difficult terrain made it an impossible destination for the Offerton project, so Archer sent stone into Staffordshire or to Derby. Transportation ceased for the winter of 1722 although eight pairs of millstones were made ready for Derby in the spring 'now the river there is navigable'. Daniel Defoe described how the local practice at the beginning of the 18th century was to mount two millstones on a wooden axle and wheel them together. This was possible near the quarry but not on easily damaged turnpike roads, nor was it good for the stones. Drawing them on sledges was another method of transport and there are long ruts on the hillsides above Padley that might be sledge marks. The usual practice was to engage a carrier using oxen. The list of turnpike charges shows how expensive this was in comparison with other vehicles. Eyre found a carrier who was at odds with Rotherham who would carry a pair of stones to Derby for £5; a year later Mr Elliot wanted to know if there was any more work from Highlow as he could buy a beast on good terms at that time. By 1724 the relationship between Eyre and Archer had soured and Archer's brother was living at Highlow. He discovered that Elliot, the carrier, was overcharging and that he had married into the rival Rotherham family and was working for them.

The millstone trade was subject to the vagaries of the industries it served. Demand sometimes dropped for years at a time. William Archer's newly engaged stone merchant was unable to sell any of his stones and Ben Ashton and Samuel Rotherham were engaged in a price war to shift their stock. Blue-black Cullen stone was being imported

53 *Covered slag heaps in the foreground mark the site of bole furnaces used for lead smelting near Mitchell Field Farm.*

by the end of the 17th century because it was considered better for grinding grain. French stones, imported as early as 1587, would eventually in the late 1700s dominate the market.

The Rotherhams were still working Millstone Edge Quarry in 1743 when the Duke of Devonshire bought the lordship of Hathersage from his relation the Duke of Newcastle. It was reported to him that the lease on Millstone Edge Quarry was to run for three more years although in fact the Eyres stayed until 1751. Although 'it is a monstrous large rock of half a mile in length and affords stone proper to make millstones', the quarry had declined in value in 1755, when quarrymasters, the Watsons, were paying a reduced rent, and under the Lowes in 1790 there is an enigmatic reference to the decline of the quarry. In 1792 Richard Oddy engaged to pay £60 a year but he could not keep up the payments, blaming present ills on past mismanagement and writing, 'not more than seventy pairs have been sold in the last ten years'. He predicted that sales would not improve 'since French Stone came into England' under a licence during the French Wars. Eventually a reduced rent of £35 was agreed with the Duke's agent.

There was a slight improvement in local stone sales during the Napoleonic Wars, but in the 19th century grit millstones were only used for animal feed. Large rings were created for the 'whims', the circles with a crushing stone to break up lead ore, while crushed stone continued to be sold for road surfacing. The industry began to fail when grinding with emery stone was introduced in 1908 and stone could be constructed artificially on or near the site of use.

Working with stone dust had always been injurious to workers' lungs. The millstone industry was virtually at an end when the Workmen's Compensation Acts of 1925-6 made employers liable for harm done to health at work. Many stones lie abandoned on the Hathersage moors, useless and too heavy to shift. Some are still with their masons' marks and give an insight into how stone was prepared.

The Callow Field Cupola

Lead was extracted to the west of Hathersage, where there was a long tradition of smelting by means either of bole or wind furnaces on the steep hillsides named after them. Using the draught from prevailing winds, the furnaces burnt fuel from the local woodlands. In the 18th and 19th centuries, however, a new method of smelting was adopted with the introduction of the cupola, a low-arched reverbatory furnace. John Farey, writing in 1811, commented that cupolas were used exclusively to smelt lead by giving the intense heat needed to expel sulphur and arsenic. Reheating with waste slag gave a lower grade lead and white slag could be used for roads. Cupolas using coal and coke were able to produce large quantities of lead ore continuously. For the first time fuel was not mixed with the ore but kept separate, thus producing a higher quality of lead and allowing temperature control. Stone-arched flue tunnels ran along or just below ground for hundreds of feet, doubling back on themselves to draw the draught toward the tall chimney needed to generate heat and conduct the poisonous fumes away from the workers. At Brough near Bradwell in the Hope Valley it is possible to see the remains of the stone flues on the hillside above today's industrial site.

Two big companies, the London Lead Company and a company of Quakers in Wales, introduced the first cupolas into Derbyshire, but it is thought that a company called Bagshaw, Twigg and Barker built Callow Field Cupola half a mile east of Hathersage, as well as the one at Ringinglow. Little is known about the cupola at Callow Bank on the exposed slopes above Mitchell Field Farm. Farey mentioned that the cupola, established after 1737 and probably nearer 1745, was occupied and worked by William Longsdon

54 *Part of a long run of underground cupola flues at Brough.*

in the late 18th century and by Joseph Storr after him. By 1802 this Joseph Storr, also running Upper Cupola in Middleton in the Dale, was paying wages and bills for coal and coke, although these must have been outstanding debts because he had died in 1801. In 1817 Thomas Birds, a descendant of William Longsdon, owned Callow Field Cupola and in 1820 William Cooke held it. As a smelter working at the cupola back in 1802, Cooke had been paid a higher price for his lead because of its quality. The high chimney helped disperse the fumes but fines were paid to farmers within a quarter of a mile to compensate for the poisoned herbage, vegetation and woodland. By the mid-1820s the Callow Field Cupola, like many others, had closed. It was described in the Award of 1830 as the 'old cupola' when the Enclosure Commissioners nominated a 'foot road' from the site up to the branch turnpike above Whim Corner.

Callow Cupola was probably too small an operation for large profits but the problem of bringing in cheap coal also contributed to its closure. John Farey described the coal measures outcropping in a long curve from Belper to Moscar which brought coal shales to the surface. There was coal at Ringinglow, collieries at Banner Cross and Greystones on the edge of Sheffield, and a coal pit at Stanage a mile from Stanage Pole. Another pit was one and a half miles to the north-east of Hathersage. The nearest coal was at White Path Moss and a tantalising reference by the Enclosure Commissioners suggests that they were 'worried about Hathersage because coal might fall into improper hands as at White Path Moss'. But these local surface pits yielded little coal and were soon exhausted. Most cupolas had closed by the 1860s as the lead industry declined, and the final blow came in 1885 with the new competition from the Broken Hill Proprietary Lead Company in Australia.

The Waltons, Maltsters of Hathersage

The Walton malt kiln with its 18th-century red bricks can still be seen in the grounds of Hathersage Hall Farm. It is often mistaken for a dovecote, which it may have been at some time in its life, but it has the classic malt house shape with a louvred roof vent to extract hot air. It had the space to accommodate the large malting floors high in the

55 *The Walton malt kiln in Hathersage Hall grounds.*

building, where barley would be steeped and laid out in a warm humid atmosphere before sifting. A wide carriageway, which is still there, sloping down to the furnace area, was used to bring coal and take away the dry malt cereal. The Walton family was living in Hathersage by the 1760s, when a James Walton was a homager in the court baron. The Walton men were respected and given full title of 'Mr Walton' in various land value lists. They left Hathersage Hall in the 1780s but were included on Land Tax lists into the 19th century, living elsewhere in Hathersage. A descendant by the name of Amorous Walton needed the Hearse in 1835. Another William Walton, a wire-drawer, was living with two other tenants at Nether Hall in 1841 and in 1856 two later Waltons were machinists in the cotton mill in Bamford.

56 *Typical interior of a malt house with barley being dried at high temperatures. The furnace is below. The usual louvred vent in the roof only collapsed in Walton's kiln in the 1990s.*

Metal Button Making

Aikin in 1795 described an old button mill in the Dale in what to him seemed a poor village. The mill was described as already in decline, but the Furniss family were to engage in button making over another seventy years on various sites, including a workshop that once stood near Back Lane in an earlier configuration of Booth Lane (now the main Sheffield Road). In an age of war, there was a ready market for metal buttons for military uniforms. A map of the 1830s shows brass casting shops associated with button making in the main street. Behind the present NatWest Bank there is a building bearing the initials of Thomas and Ann Furniss and dated 1781 that was a workshop for the family's button-making activities before 1833 when it had become a house.

Chapter 23

The New Turnpike Roads

In the 18th century it was possible for men of business to form a Turnpike Trust by a private Act of Parliament. Such a trust would be responsible for the maintenance of local stretches of turnpike road through charges on vehicles passing the tollhouse. The lists of the petitioners for such an Act and later subscribers include virtually all the great names of any parish. There were hundreds of such Acts in the 18th century and three of them concerned Hathersage. The earliest created the Sparrowpit Turnpike Trust of 1758. This was responsible for a road from Highfield in Sheffield, through Ringinglow and over Burbage Brook, then passing down the Dale along the main street of Hathersage, and on to Castleton and westward via Sparrowpit to Stockport. It had been planned to take it past the new Callow Field Cupola, but this was abandoned above the cupola because the higher slopes are convex and coaches and wagons would never have made the gradient.

The ideal turnpike was 40 feet wide to avoid affording shelter for highwaymen. It was well made, with a camber and ditch to assist drainage. In reality, though, toll roads were often primitive and poorly made, their construction slow and done in stages, often

57 The original 1758 turnpike road peters out on convex slopes. The cupola was sited above Callow Farm, seen here.

58 *The Sparrowpit turnpike of 1758 detoured in the 1760s to use easier slopes. Callow Farm is just out of view to the right.*

59 *The tollbooth is half a mile from the village on the present Sheffield Road. The Sparrowpit Turnpike Trust completed the last stretch of the planned Greenhill turnpike in 1825.*

not on the routes first considered. Road planners commonly ignored gradients and difficult terrain often required later changes of direction. Some turnpikes were never built or were left unfinished.

Individual Turnpike Acts had a time limitation and annual renewals were granted by Parliament. In the years following 1758 the Dale section of the Sparrowpit Turnpike was redirected, circling Callow Field to the north before heading eastward toward Overstones, Burbage Brook and on to Sheffield. The road never reached the requirements of a turnpike and there was a petition in 1795 against the renewal of the Act. The old turnpike had lost its status by the time the branch turnpike of 1811 was built from Whim Corner to Burbage Brook.

The Greenhill Moor Trust had been brought into existence in 1781 to turnpike the route from Greenhill Moor near Chesterfield, via Holmesfield, Owler Bar and *Fox House Inn*, to Hathersage. The intention was that the road should descend the steep slopes below Millstone Edge to join another turnpike road at Leadmill by the River Derwent, but in reality the road from *Fox House Inn* westward was nothing more than a track and

60 *The old Mortimer Road route here passed close to Leach House until 1926.*

the last two miles of road were never built. The 1811 Sparrowpit Branch Turnpike and proposed Greenhill Turnpike roads would have run close to each other at Hathersage Booths, causing unmanageable difficulties, but the problem was resolved when an Act of 1825 gave the Sparrowpit Turnpike Trust powers to build the unfinished section of road from *Fox House* to Hathersage, taking all future profits, but an explicit order stated that no tollhouse and bar was to be built between the two places. This condition is at odds with the fact that a tollhouse was built and still stands on the Sheffield Road, half a mile out of the village. It may have replaced the earlier tollgate at a junction near Hathersage Hall at the bottom of the hill, which disappeared during an earlier realignment. The great achievement in this section was the cutting of a way through what is now known as the Surprise View at Millstone Edge. James Holworthy, a new resident in 1825, made a special note of it in his Commonplace Book and listed the money due to its road makers.

Another road, later known as Mortimer Road, passed through Hathersage. A trust was formed in 1771 to connect Grindleford with Penistone, part of an even grander plan to link Bakewell with York to assist the local textile trade. This was the idea of Hans Winthrop Mortimer, the great landowner of

61 *The toll bar at Mytham Bridge has been preserved.*

62 *The Surprise View. The route was opened though the rocks in 1825 by the Sparrowpit Turnpike Trust.*

Bamford and the main subscriber, although supported by Mr Oxley of Leam. The work cost a fortune and bankrupted Mortimer in 1807. The grandiose project was never completed but a section from Grindleford through Hathersage to Bamford was built. There was careful consideration as to where the tollhouse with its obligatory lamp should be sited and, according to early maps, it was marked close to the present *Plough Inn*. Another turnpike bar was proposed at Mytham Bridge near Bamford, because it had long been agreed that there must be 'no turnpike between Mytham Bridge and the malt house in the possession of James Walton in the village of Hathersage or any part of the said village'. William Walton had been one of the original petitioners and subscribers and his son feared incurring extra charges on the transport of his malt. As with all turnpikes, though, there were exemptions to charges, and John Shuttleworth and some farmers were granted free passage for their corn and cereals at the Leadmill tollhouse. Although Mortimer's Road was extended from Mytham Bridge to Bamford in 1826, and other sections to the north were built, the whole road was never completed. The fate of the local section appears in the introduction to a later Petition: 'Whereas the road leading from the bottom of Hathersage over Hazelford Bridge through Fall Cliff Woods to Grindleford Bridge is in a bad condition and cannot be sufficiently repaired and maintained by the ordinary course of law, it would be advantageous to the public and inhabitants if the said road was placed under the Sparrowpit Trustees.' This came to pass.

Later Acts of Parliament consolidated trusts to bring various roads under one authority. Challenged by the advent of railways, turnpikes had mostly disappeared well before the 1880s when the new local councils took over the maintenance of roads in their area. Hathersage would wait until 1894 for a railway to come through and it missed canals altogether.

Chapter 24

Hathersage Hall

At the top of the main street in Hathersage stands Hathersage Hall, a graceful residence set in serene gardens close to its farm. Although the date stone on its east wall says 1495, much of the Hall today dates from the 17th century, when Robert Ashton of Stoney Middleton transformed it from a farmstead to a gentleman's residence. Robert Ashton (1610–87), a wealthy merchant who made a fortune from extracting and working lead, had avoided taking sides in the Civil Wars but when in 1662 Charles II requested a list of 'how gentlemen of Derbyshire were affected [in the Civil Wars] and fit to lend money to the king', Ashton was declared to be worth £10,000 a year and able to lend £6,000. If he did so it may explain his appointment as High Sheriff in 1664 and Justice of the Peace in 1673. He became important in Hathersage as a landowner and ancestor of the present Shuttleworth family.

Over a 40-year period he spent thousands of pounds buying land in north Derbyshire, and his will of 1683 was complex, providing for the children of three wives. After his death in 1687, Benjamin, his son by the third wife, inherited the Hathersage estates and property in Bradwell, Aston and Hope. He lived in Hathersage Hall with his wife Christiana Turner and their eight children. Little is known of him except that in 1691 he became a trustee of the charity known as the Hathersage Vicar and Poor of Stoney Middleton, and his signature appears as a witness to the accuracy of the Hathersage churchwardens' accounts from 1689. His son, also named Benjamin, inherited at his father's death in 1717. This Benjamin who endowed the school at Geer Green was not the eldest son, but all his brothers predeceased their father. His obesity was a matter of comment at the time. On one occasion in 1721 he thanked William Archer for allowing him to drive his coach through the Highlow estate to take the air at Abney. He died in 1725 and is buried in Hathersage parish church.

His only remaining sister had made a fortunate alliance by marrying William Spencer of Cannon Hall near Barnsley. The Spencers were descended from John Spencer of Criggon, Montgomeryshire, who had made a fortune in Yorkshire by converting bolehill operations

63 *Hall Farm buildings date from 1841 when Hathersage Hall was restored after it was damaged by a fire in that year.*

to charcoal blast furnaces over the period 1650 to 1690, and his business partnership with Major Walter Spencer dominated the iron industry in the early 18th century from Leeds to Staveley. The first Spencer of Cannon Hall was John

64 Ashton Ashton Shuttleworth and his first wife Sarah Flinn. Her hair and dress suggests a date in the 1780s.

Spencer of Barnby Furnace, who was 'much engaged in minerals'. He married the widow of the owner in the late 17th century, bought his stepdaughter's interest and, to add to his mineral activities, found coal on the estate. In 1715 William Spencer, John's son, married the Ashton heiress, Christiana Ashton, inheriting Hathersage Hall on Benjamin Ashton's death in 1725. Four years later his own father died, giving him two estates to run. William and Christiana Spencer lived at Cannon Hall but made long visits to Hathersage where William involved himself in village affairs.

On the death of their mother, Christiana, the eldest daughter took over the task of running the household and ten children. Her letters tell us much about life at the time. She is surprised that 'cupping' has not relieved her father's rheumatism and comments on a 'handsome' funeral where mourners were given shawls and gloves. Food and drink mentioned includes gifts of venison and other meats. Tea was expensive and welcomed as a present, Christiana asking her father to bring Twining's tea when he returned from London. A relation, who died in 1774 by falling on a fire while rendering fat, is said never to have drunk tea or coffee in her life. A delivery to Hathersage Hall of a block of sugar provides a delightful picture of the family cutting pieces from it.

In 1748 there were two weddings from Cannon Hall, Christiana marrying Captain William Shuttleworth of the 7th Royal Fusiliers and her sister, Ann Spencer, marrying Walter Stanhope of Leeds. When William Spencer died in 1756 their brother John inherited Cannon Hall and Hathersage Hall. Aged 38, a lawyer and Batchelor of the Middle Temple who lived the life of a dandy in London, he found managing his inheritance – the business affairs of the Spencer coalmines near Cannon Hall and the quarrying and lead interests of the Ashtons around Hathersage – tedious. Gradually he became more adjusted to life as a squire but Hathersage Hall saw little of him and was eventually leased to a tenant. When he died in 1775 the estates were divided between his two nephews, Walter Spencer Stanhope and John Shuttleworth. After legal fine-tuning, Stanhope inherited Cannon Hall and Shuttleworth received the Hathersage estate.

Christiana and William Shuttleworth travelled with the 7th Fusiliers, their children born wherever the regiment was stationed. In his early life William had the money difficulties of a young officer seeking promotion in the 18th century. John Spencer was generous to his sister Christiana and paid for the education of her sons, later purchasing, as was the custom, their commissions in the Army. The two senior sons, John and Ashton Shuttleworth, who would inherit the Hathersage estate in turn, were posted to North America in the early 1770s and wrote occasionally to their uncle. John was 'disappointed' in Quebec and thought Hathersage 'quite a Palace' by comparison. In 1772 Ashton was in New York and was clearly critical of the social assemblies there. Long Island he found was barren but good for shooting and hunting and there was a fine bird called a Mocking Bird. He warned that there would be a 'noise' soon about tea from England being taxed, but Americans would get it illegally from Holland. In fact, this was the provocation that led to the outbreak of the War of American Independence from 1776 to 1782.

Ashton served throughout the war, from the Battles of Lexington and Bunker Hill to Brandywine Creek, the battle that led to the British capture of Philadelphia. In the terrible winter of 1777-8 he was transferred to Nova Scotia, now in danger of attack by the French who supported the colonials. He was stationed in Halifax and remained there for most of the duration of the war.

His elder brother, John Shuttleworth, a Lieutenant in the 13th Royal Fusiliers, had become a prisoner of war when Burgoyne's army was trapped on the way down the River Hudson. With seventy other captives he was marched to the famous Fort Ticonderoga and later Trenton. There is a stoical silence in his letters about the discomforts caused by the distances he was travelling. After an exchange of prisoners he was stationed on Staten Island while the war swept southward. By now a Captain, he returned in 1777 to London where his father, Captain William Shuttleworth, aged 67, came to meet him.

At the end of the war Ashton Shuttleworth was given the sensitive mission of retrieving English arms and ammunition from a frontier fort on the Penobscott River and bringing them back to Nova Scotia. His journey downriver in the depths of winter gave rise to problems with storms, incompetent pilots and, finally, the ship running aground. The supplies had to be jettisoned to let the ship float free. With the likelihood of an inquiry into such an ill-fated journey, Ashton wisely kept records of what happened.

Six months later, back in Halifax, Nova Scotia, Ashton married Miss Sarah Flinn in July 1784. By 1786 his regiment had returned from Canada to Woolwich, the headquarters of the Royal Artillery, but his parents were dead. He was close to his younger brother, Edmund, who had a less distinguished military career, and he went to see Edmund embark from the Solent to join his new regiment in India where he was to die. Ashton described the departure and recorded his death in his mother's prayer book.

65 *Hathersage Hall, the early home of the Shuttleworth family, seen here c.1865.*

66 *Col. A.J. Shuttleworth to the right with some of his staff at Nether Hall, c.1909.*

67 *Nether Hall, the present home of the Shuttleworth family, was built by 1842.*

John Shuttleworth had inherited Hathersage Hall and estate in 1775 while he was in America and could not attend to his affairs. His cousin, Walter Spencer Stanhope, was the trustee who watched over his interests for most of the 19 years of his tenure of the Hathersage estate. Christiana and William Shuttleworth, living in Chesterfield, had complained to John in America that Stanhope was letting the Hall become ruinous and the trees overgrown, but their anxieties were probably overstated for the maltster, William Walton, was living in Hathersage Hall in John's absence. John was later to serve in Scotland, Gibraltar and Quebec, visiting Hathersage only occasionally. In 1793 he was clearly unwell and wanted to sell his commission to James, his youngest brother. He died in Chesterfield on 8 July 1794 and is buried in Hathersage parish church. His brother Ashton Ashton Shuttleworth inherited. A friend and neighbour at Leam Hall was Marmaduke Middleton Middleton, another variation on fashionable double naming.

In 1793 the French Revolutionary War had begun and Ashton was on active service in the Netherlands with the Duke of York's army when he inherited the estate. He could do little about his inheritance for by October he was with the army near Grossbach, under the thunder of a cannonade and about to take seven hundred wagons across the River Waal. Sarah was in Portsmouth preparing to join him. Ashton told her to sell the horses and send their china, carefully wrapped, by stagecoach to Hathersage Hall. She had a draft on a Portsmouth bank and could leave her gold watch there. She should bring a blue riding dress and a side saddle and leave her parrot behind with a friend. There is no evidence that this intrepid lady made the journey before the army withdrew. At the end of 1795 Ashton's health broke down and he left the Army on full pay. By 1796, at the age of 41, Ashton was in residence in Hathersage where he remained for the next 35 years. He is the direct ancestor of the present Shuttleworth family.

Chapter 25

Squire Ashton

Ashton's health improved in Hathersage and he took his position of squire of Hathersage Hall seriously, although spending, by his own admission, much time and money on horses and hunting. He honoured the charity willed by Ben Ashton for Geer Green School in 1718 and the Sylvester charity charge to a property he now owned. He viewed the new vicar, Le Cornu, with dissatisfaction and began to keep a record of his shortcomings: there was only one Sunday service in winter and that was at 2p.m.; Le Cornu had refused the Sacrament to Henry Ibbotson and John Bunting on their deathbeds, presumably because they were Wesleyans; his clerk was drunk and unruly in a service.

Nothing could have prepared Sarah Shuttleworth for life in Hathersage after her travels in Canada and garrisons in England. Ashton was away from the Hall much of the time and on one occasion he brought home two orphans of a former Army servant. A son was born in 1801 and named after his father. In December 1806 Sarah and Ashton had bid farewell to a visitor when Sarah, returning indoors first, 'went upstairs and laid on the floor and died'; so James, her brother-in-law and greatly affected, wrote to his cousin. She is buried in the family vault in Hathersage church.

Ashton's younger brother James had been destined for an apprenticeship in the cotton trade until the War of American Independence so depressed trade that he eagerly followed his brothers into the Army. Taking his brother John's commission he became a Captain in the Royal Fusiliers, his father's old regiment. By 1796 he was spending much time at Hathersage Hall, still hoping for preferment. In 1799 he waited two hours to be received by Prince Edward, the colonel of his regiment, in order to present his 'memorial'. Although he was referred to another colonel, nothing more is heard of James' attempt to continue in the Army. He was 45 and too old for advancement so he settled in Hathersage where he involved himself in village and family affairs. He was a member of the Hathersage Association for the Prosecution of Felons, a society of gentlemen devised to keep local order in an age when only a constable maintained the peace. He was interested in the Little John legends and collected the supposed relics that were dug up at that time. He and his cousin kept them until, after a run of bad luck, James restored his trophy to the church and Cannon Hall lost the rest. He followed closely the family claims in the enclosure of the wastes after 1808. He encouraged Ashton to become a magistrate and dabbled inaccurately with the family tree. Married to Elizabeth Heath, a widow, he lived at Stoney Middleton until his death in 1829 while visiting Barnes Hall in Ecclesfield.

Ashton remarried in 1807, this time to Anne Youle and was transformed. He turned over a new leaf, hunted less and sold some of his horses. After a penurious childhood and the privations of army life, he was now a family man of substance and a great landowner. Nine children were born but of the boys only John Spencer Ashton Shuttleworth, born in 1817, lived to manhood.

Ashton commanded the somewhat reluctant local militia in the years 1803–5 when invasion by Napoleon threatened. He often chaired the annual vestry meetings dealing with church and secular matters in the parish and was one of the petitioners with the Duke of Devonshire in 1808 for an Act for the enclosure of wastes and commons in Hathersage. He took part in meetings with the enclosure commissioners and attended their land auctions but never saw the fruits of his work as he died just after the Award was made in 1830.

He had a keen interest in turnpikes, and in 1808 he built the *Ordnance Arms* as a coaching inn in anticipation of the 1811 branch turnpike at Whim Corner and another planned link with the Duke of Devonshire's turnpike past *Fox House Inn* to Sheffield, which was only finished in 1825. The *Ordnance Arms* lay empty for some years and took time to become established. When canals became popular Ashton attended a meeting of local gentlemen to hear Thomas Telford, the great canal builder, on the possibility of a canal from Abbeydale in Sheffield to Edale in the Hope Valley. He was also an employer in most of the local industries. He had quarries and was a partner in lead mines in the area, especially at Eyam and Foolow. In Hathersage one of his tenants, Joseph Pearson, had for a time run a cotton workshop on Hood Brook, and the wire manufacturers were tenants on his land.

In 1824 Ashton befriended a newcomer to the village when he sold him Brookfield together with 70 acres of land. James Holworthy of Leicestershire was a wealthy gentleman who had married a niece of Joseph Wright, the celebrated painter of Derby. Holworthy had no allotment from the Enclosure Award apart from a consortium claim relating to Moscar House Farm. He set about transforming the old Brookfield farm and cottages into a hall. Later he was to create a vast estate by buying nearly three hundred acres from those who wished to sell their allotments and the commissioners obligingly arranged a rerouting of the road in the vicinity of Brookfield to his advantage.

Holworthy had been a member of the newly formed Water Colour Society in London and today his work is preserved in the Tate Britain Gallery, the National Art Library and the hands of private collectors. He had known the *belle monde* of London society, attending soirées, exhibitions and art galleries, and sometimes travelled throughout Britain finding scenes to draw and meeting possible patrons. He came to know J.M.W. Turner and their letters to each other reflect a deepening friendship.

Holworthy did not paint after he arrived in Hathersage although he kept in touch with his patron, the Duke of Rutland. Turner wrote several letters to Holworthy teasing him about his new role as a great landowner and promising to visit him one day. The visit never took place but the two continued to meet in London. Turner enquired twice after Holworthy's hands so it is possible that rheumatism or some other ailment prevented him from painting. Neverthless, he was able to conduct business and would act later as guardian to Ashton's young family and serve as a magistrate.

No two could be more different than Ashton Shuttleworth and his new friend James Holworthy. Ashton was 70 and Holworthy 46 when they met, Ashton a man of action and an old soldier and Holworthy an aesthete who complained of Ashton's disinterest in antiquities. Despite this they struck up a firm friendship, dining together, strolling in the woods away from the 'hateful' mills in the village and sending each other presents of game. With no children of his own, Holworthy enjoyed Ashton's young family and was interested in his family history. On one occasion Holworthy stayed so long at Hathersage Hall that in the dark he would have fallen in the brook on the way back to Brookfield 'but for my Lanthorn', and his wife rebuked him for his late return.

It is from Holworthy's Commonplace Book that we get some idea of the shadows clouding Ashton's last days. In October 1828 his second daughter died of tuberculosis.

Alicia was 26 years of age and had been sent to lodgings in Sheffield away from the younger children to be nursed by her elder sister, Christiana, who herself would die three years later. Much saddened by Alicia's death, Holworthy wrote a fulsome eulogy for this charming and unaffected girl. In the same month of his daughter's death, Ashton witnessed an accident as he passed the open doorway of a Hathersage mill. He saw one of his servants, Samuel Higginbottom, trapped in the cogs of the huge wheel; he was crushed to death in front of Ashton, who was deeply upset. Then his brother James Shuttleworth died in 1829, leaving Ashton the sole remaining son of Christiana.

Ashton died on 9 July 1830, 13 days after the long awaited Enclosure Award and a fortnight after the death of George IV, and is buried in the family vault in Hathersage parish church. His life spanned two ages: he lived through the great days of the two William Pitts, he witnessed the social and industrial changes of the 18th century and fought in the American and French Wars; he also saw the transformation of Hathersage from a 'poor empty village with a button works' of the 1790s to a place with links to the outside world, a new school and the beginning of an industrial future. He was a conscientious squire whose long life gave his family 36 years to settle in the village. In 1838 his heir, the young John Shuttleworth, bought Nether Hall homestead and land and built a residence there in the early 1840s, but the family continued to live in Hathersage Hall in the mid-20th century.

As executor of Ashton's will and guardian of his young family, James Holworthy proved a careful administrator until his guardianship ended in 1839. He resumed his visits to London and was there when the census of June 1841 was taken. He never returned to his home for he was taken ill there and died at the *Osborne Hotel* in the Adelphi area of London close to today's Embankment. He is buried in Kensal Green Cemetery.

James Holworthy preserved the old notes and papers left by Ashton Shuttleworth, having a nostalgic admiration for Ashton's long family history. Ashton's heir, John Spencer Ashton Shuttleworth, had an even longer sojourn than that of his father. All Ashton's descendants would follow military careers in the war zones of the 19th and 20th centuries, serving in the RAF and Navy. Squadron Leader Richard Shuttleworth was shot down over Amsterdam in 1941 and Commander John Shuttleworth served in the Navy, seeing action in Korea in the 1950s. Three of his sons served in the Navy and one in the Army. Michael Shuttleworth, the senior son, was in the Royal Marines for 12 years, seeing service in the Far East, and he acted for the Foreign Office as an observer in Yugoslavia in the 1990s. Members of the family also worked locally on councils and committees and as Justices of the Peace. There is a memorial lamp in the centre of the village and a path to the church from Baulk Lane dedicated to the memory of members of the family.

Chapter 26

The Enclosures

As the Industrial Revolution gained momentum in the 18th century the growing urban population needed more food. Prices rose for grains loosely referred to as corn, and landowners were keen to take advantage of this lucrative commodity, especially in the French Revolutionary and Napoleonic Wars when foreign corn was unavailable. Selective breeding of farm animals to increase their size had been practised since the days of Robert Bakewell, and Viscount Townsend had pioneered the growing of turnips to feed cattle through the winter to maintain the size of the herds. These practices, and new tools like Tull's horse-drawn hoe and the Rotherham plough, were not suited to the open fields of England, with their numerous strips and cultivators, while grazing on common land would not produce pedigree animals. Intensive farming needed more enclosures on wasteland.

Around Hathersage, old enclosures were extensive. Neighbours had made private agreements to exchange land to make more compact plots. In 1808 the Duke of Devonshire, as lord of the manor, had a private Bill to enclose the wastes and commons of Hathersage prepared. His fellow petitioners included all the old gentry of the area, John Balguy of Hope and Derwent, Joseph Denman MD of Derwent, Ashton Ashton Shuttleworth of Hathersage and Padley and John Le Cornu, vicar of Hathersage, among others.

The resulting Act included the usual conditions. The great landowners' rights were protected, even the king, as Duke of Lancaster, retaining his 'palfrey silver'. The Duke of Devonshire kept his mining rights. Tithes, manorial and ecclesiastic, were commuted to rents. The change was such an integral part of the Enclosure Award that there is no Tithe Map for Hathersage. A Justice of the Peace was to inspect the commissioners' accounts. Proprietors were to pay for the assigned walling or fencing of their new allotments as well as other fees. New land was to be held according to the assignee's existing tenure.

The commissioners were named as James Dowland of Cuckney and John Nuttall of Matlock with William Gauntley of Bakewell as Umpire. When Dowland died in 1823, George Unwin of Whitwell was sworn in by the Duke of Devonshire to replace him. All the commissioners were experienced surveyors and their impartiality was assured because they were not local. They chose a bank in Chesterfield, Crompton, Walker and Co., to deal with the considerable sums of money involved. They employed Joseph and William Fairbank, surveyors of Sheffield, to do the actual measuring and charting and their papers, plans and maps are still available. William Cheek of Tideswell became their attorney.

Progress was slow and the Award was not made until June 1830. The commissioners met once or twice a year although at times of peak activity they met once a month at inns not always near Hathersage. The freeholders of Hathersage once complained about the distant meeting places, suspecting intrigue, but there was a simpler explanation: Dowland, Nuttall and later Unwin travelled long distances from their homes and met at their own convenience or near disputed boundaries. To meet claimants of the new allotments or those with grievances, special meetings were often held at the *George* in Hathersage where, in the past, inquests, manorial courts and post mortems had been held. At other times they met at the *Ordnance Arms*, in the main street close to the *George*, the *Peacock* at Baslow, the *Moon* at Stoney Middleton and the *Angel* in Sheffield to name but a few venues.

The first practical concern was to raise money to pay fees to the commissioners, the Fairbanks and William Cheek and to cover expenses. Accordingly land auctions were held to sell off outlying parcels of land. In 1809 land round Longshaw reached high prices, as did land abutting turnpikes, but in the auction of August 1819 there were no buyers.

An early stage of the commissioners' work was to map existing roads, examine their status and give authority for new roads or private carriageways as were deemed necessary. Their remit also covered bridges and drains. With the consent of two Justices, they could divert, stop up, discontinue, alter or change any public carriageway, private road or footpath leading through private or old enclosures. They defined five categories of road, ranging from 40ft-wide public carriageways to 6ft-wide foot roads as at Cupola. By October 1819 the roads were proclaimed and the map showing them was ready. A few extra private roads were announced in the *Derby Mercury* in January 1823 and a diversion of Coggers Lane was made as late as 1829.

Public quarries were to be available to new proprietors to acquire stone to build the necessary walling round their plots. These quarries were on land belonging to the petitioners and a charge would be made for the stone taken. Eleven were designated for public use although the owner of each plot kept right of herbage. Up to 10 acres was set aside for public watering places for beasts, as well as a few areas to burn limestone and collect sand and gravel for houses, walls, bridges and repair of roads.

In 1811 a perambulation was made with overseers from neighbouring parishes to agree boundaries. That same year claims were invited from those holding old enclosure land to apply for an allotment (allocation) on the commons and wastes. By 1814 such claims would require written proof of ownership. By 1817 there was a comprehensive list of all owners and tenants, with numbers given to their old enclosures and property in and around the village. A Draft Map of the proposed new allotments was also drawn up and a Book of Claims was exhibited at the *George Inn* and at Derwent. Objections were invited the next year.

In addition to the painstaking measuring, mapping and recording, the commissioners adjudicated in disputes. Extraordinary meetings were held with the petitioners present to discuss the boundary dispute with Dore Parish which dated back to the previous century. It was finally resolved in 1818. Hathersage land to the north-east bordered the Duke of Norfolk's Hallamdale property, enclosed since the 1790s. The Duke had not fenced his land appropriately and it affected that owned by James Holworthy. It also affected White Path Moss, where the coal pit had caused the commissioners concern. Legal proceedings began against the Duke and the issue was not resolved until 1826.

Two of the petitioners came into dispute with the commissioners. The Duke of Devonshire made a claim on Highlow to the west of the River Derwent that was disallowed by the commissioners, and Ashton Ashton Shuttleworth claimed lordship of the manor of Padley. The 1808 Act referred to him as 'lord of the manor of the reputed manor of Padley'. This aspiration seems to have begun during his ancestor Benjamin Ashton's tenure in the 1690s and great store was set by the title, but the manor itself did not exist. There was a romantic tendency in the 19th century to admire ancient titles and promote what had been a farm to a hall, and a hall to a manor. Padley had never been a manor in Domesday Book and the occasional Perambulations, one of which

68 *Scraperlow House, once on the edge of the commons, is still a local landmark above Booths. The figures suggest a date of 1787.*

Ashton's brother John had attended, showed that the Baslow and Hathersage boundaries met at Padley. The one-time residence of the Fitzherberts at Padley was in Hathersage manor and parish. The Duke decided in 1819 to challenge the commissioners on both claims, however, and summoned them to a hearing at Edensor with Justices present. At what must have been an intimidating occasion, the commissioners stuck to their guns and the Duke and Ashton both lost their claims.

It was clear by 1822 that Mr Dowland was ill. He had missed meetings that year and never attended again. He died in August 1823 and it was over four months before Mr Unwin was sworn in by the Duke of Devonshire; he had worked with Dowland on other enclosures and had just finished work on the Dore enclosure.

The more formal paper work began with the Instruction of Award in 1824, and by 1825 a Draft of the Award was ready although it was still receiving finishing touches in January 1828. By then commissioners' accounts were in arrears and they were asking proprietors to pay their debts. A deadline for payment was fixed for 30 May and in October the commissioners held one last meeting at the *Angel Inn* in Sheffield to submit their final accounts and expenses to Justice of the Peace Marmaduke Middleton Middleton of Leam. The Award was announced on 27 June 1830 at Divine Service in the parish church. William IV, the third king since the enclosure process began, had ruled for less than 24 hours.

Hathersage enclosure covering 10,000 acres had taken much longer than usual as the commissioners were working on other enclosures at the same time. This was only possible because they delegated work to local surveyors like the Fairbanks. Legal disputes and the death of Commissioner Dowland had added to the complexity of their work.

After all the claims of would-be proprietors had been examined, only 50 people were entitled to the 158 allotments, some vast and others quite small. A plot was identified by naming neighbours' allotments on all sides or sometimes by indicating a road next to it. Each owner was responsible for building clearly defined walls that had to be six feet high and two feet wide at the base. Not all owners with small allotments could afford the walling costs and commissioners' fees so they sold their plots even before the Award was final.

It is tempting to believe that there was a rush to occupy and wall each allotment, since walling had to be complete by 1 November. Realistically, though, it would have been impossible in that time to cart stones to remote holdings. Fifty proprietors could not use the quarries over such a short period and continue their usual occupations. The process had to be more gradual and it is likely that from 1817 groups of neighbours made tentative plans to identify and use their plots wherever they presented no challenge. By 1822 Rhodes mentioned the new walls he saw on his travels.

Although the wastes and commons had belonged to the lord of the manor, by long custom he had allowed certain people to graze beasts on them. The limitations were often ignored and others grazed animals there too. Now the new fields were closed. The poor villager had no common land available for grazing or cutting turf for his fire. He would not be able to keep animals and grow crops on his croft in the village. In many cases men were driven from the land to find work in towns or became farm labourers for wealthier landowners. The enclosures created a social upheaval that accentuated the class distinction between labourers and gentry at a time when the Whig reforms of the 1830s led to franchises based on property and the Union Workhouse for the destitute.

Chapter 27

The Textile Connection

Although other villages in north Derbyshire are better known for textile working, Hathersage too has its place. In the 17th century flax and hemp had been grown and worked there. Uniquely it made the hacklepins for combs necessary to prepare flax, silk, cotton or wool for spinning. Spinning was a very common domestic labour done by women from local villages for clothiers often from Manchester of Macclesfield and Hathersage was no exception. Weaving was a job for men and their looms were usually situated on the top floor of cottages whose windows under the eaves provided the necessary extra light.

In the 18th century the growing population and fashion for cotton encouraged merchants to import more. They created such a volume of raw cotton that ways had to be found to mechanise processing. Individual efforts to produce knitting frames and spinning and weaving machines began in the 1730s and new devices were invented to harmonise the output during the rest of the century.

Most of the early machines were intended for use in workers' homes but inventors and clothiers soon preferred to keep the machines safe in workshops, even though their prototypes were sometimes smashed by workers fearful for their jobs in mill towns like Blackburn, Nottingham, Derby and Manchester. The small villages of north Derbyshire provided a safer environment for the machines, with willing workers and the necessary fast-running watercourses. An upsurge in the opening of textile mills in the region

69 *All that remains of Pearson's calico works, which became part of Tobias Child's Victoria Works in the 19th century.*

70 *Hood Brook running into the defunct mill pond that powered Pearson's and later Child's waterwheels.*

followed successful challenges in the courts to Arkwright's patents in 1785. Mills were built, or old ones adapted, at Litton, Calver, Tideswell, Eyam, Edale, Bamford, Bradwell, Brough, Great Longstone and Bakewell.

An old villager told James Holworthy that he remembered a time when there was a spinning wheel in nearly every house in Hathersage and cotton workshops were listed in 1801 and 1810. There is reference to a calico works in the village. The mill, on a site later to become the Victoria Works, was noted in the lists and plans of the old enclosures drawn up in 1817. It was owned by Ashton Ashton Shuttleworth with Joseph Pearson as his tenant, a relative of the Pearsons who had run the cotton mills at nearby Brough from 1794. The Hathersage workshop fell into disuse and the enterprise was largely forgotten but it is still a matter of record.

There are also references to weaving. In the early 18th century the Ibbotsons on the hillsides at Hurst were weavers. In 1826 James Holworthy was told that William Walton, the maltster tenant at Hathersage Hall in the 1770s, 'had his malt kiln near Henry Cocker's weaving house', and later Thomas Walton 'washed Cocker's weaving at the malt house'. It is possible that the weaving shed was in or near 'the old button mill' by Dale Brook, for another source refers to 'river tenters'. It was clearly a short-lived project but conjures up visions of cloth drying on tenterhooks somewhere in the Dale.

One of the first processes in textile working had always been to comb and draw raw cotton or wool fibres into rovings, 'tops' and, finally, strands ready for spinning. This was done with hackle combs and gills made in Hathersage. In earlier times hand hackle combs were used, but later the pins were bedded in a large block on a stand or bench. When Cartwright's 'Big Ben' machine of 1792 automated combing it still incorporated hackle pinned combs, as did later machines. Hathersage manufacturers were to become famous for the production of hackle and gill pins for these machines in the 19th century, whether designed for silk, linen, flax, wool or cotton. They were all made from wire drawn from iron or later steel rod.

Wire drawing in Hathersage has been noted as early as 1566, when a German immigrant, Christopher Schutz, set up his workshop, probably by invitation as Germans led the way in metalworking; he was closed down by a rival patenter who had influence with Queen Elizabeth. In after years Thomas Heaton of Mitchell Field was described as a wire drawer at his death in 1670, as was his grandson. Throughout the 18th and 19th centuries it was common for men to describe themselves as wire drawers.

Traditionally wire was drawn from lengths of cold iron rod by hand through a series of holes of diminishing size in 'wortle plates', gradually producing fine wire. When demand was high, this was done in Hathersage by outworkers who were farmers and villagers with other occupations. The process was supervised by steel merchants from Sheffield who controlled the annealing or heating between drawings necessary when the wire became too brittle. They would also close the wortle holes when they wore loose.

Hathersage wire came to play an important part in the old needle industry of Redditch through a connection with the Sheffield Cocker family. By 1750 Benjamin Huntsman of Sheffield was making crucible steel and in 1752 he persuaded Samuel Cocker in Sheffield to try drawing cast steel wire at his Porter Steel Works in Sharrow Vale. In 1802 William Huntsman was still using Cocker's cast steel rod for wire to send to Henry Milward, an established maker of needles in Redditch. Cocker's relations in Hathersage were often called upon to draw this wire for Huntsman and it was not long before they moved into the needle trade in their own right. Wire drawing probably played a part in the opening of the paper mill near Greens House that traded until the mid-19th century, making the thick brown paper needed to wrap industrial goods and the bundles of rod or wire for delivery to Redditch.

Chapter 28

The Needle Makers

Britain was at war with France from 1793 and by 1805 France's new Emperor, Napoleon Bonaparte, planned to invade. Admiral Nelson's victory at the Battle of Trafalgar prevented that and Britain went on to blockade European ports under French control, although many, ignoring Napoleon's ban, found ways to trade with Britain. Trade with India and the Far East continued too, but Britain's policy towards France caused war with America in 1812. It was during this period of war that far-reaching industrial changes took place in Hathersage.

Robert and David Cook

On 14 July 1811 an advertisement appeared in a local newspaper, the *Sheffield Mercury*, proclaiming that Robert and David Cook were open to business as wire drawers and makers of fish hooks, needles, hackle pins, gill pins for combing cotton, and pins for other machinery in their workshops at Hathersage. Such was the impact of this new enterprise on the village that a month later the Cockers also advertised that they were in business.

The Cook brothers had come from Studley near Redditch, a village involved in the local needle trade by the middle of the 18th century. Where the Cooks worked at first in Hathersage is unknown. They are not mentioned in the comprehensive list of properties, owners and tenants compiled in 1817-18 by the Enclosure Commissioners, but they could have been sub-tenants. Robert was 22 years old and his brother was 17 when they set up in business and by the 1820s they were established as Shuttleworth tenants in workshops with waterwheels powered by Hood Brook. The buildings, later known as Barnfield Works, were extended but the frontage seen today was added much later. Part of the works is still used and the chimney stack and boiler house, built when steam power was introduced, are still visible although the waterwheel is long gone.

The Cooks left no written explanation as to why they chose to come to Hathersage. In Redditch a system had evolved whereby a few major needle manufacturers would place work in its various processing stages with lesser workshops and private households in outlying villages. One of the employers, Henry Milward, worked from the *Fountain Inn* at Redditch, which was already the usual venue for moving half-processed needles or wire from one worker to another and exchanging money, whether for wages or sales. It was also the custom for employers to send outriders through Britain for months at a time to sell needles and find new markets. It is more than likely that the Cooks came from a family with experience of needle working and were outriders for Milward or another manufacturer and that, passing through Hathersage, they had become aware of the endless need for needles, hackle pins and gill pins at the new carding and combing machines in the nearby mills. The young Cooks saw the opening and took it. Redditch at that time did not make industrial needles, and by the time it did the Cooks were prime producers of hooks, pins and needles for a variety of textile machines in Britain and Europe. Familiar with the Sheffield steel rod and wire that had long been sent to Redditch, the Cooks were now close to their own supply, even quicker access being afforded by the new Sparrowpit Branch Turnpike also built in 1811.

In 1822, in his book *Excursions in Derbyshire*, E. Rhodes wrote of Hathersage:

> Steel wire and needles are likewise made here under the direction of men regularly initiated into the business, and in other respects competent to the undertaking. These manufactures may therefore have a more permanent duration; but establishments of this description are perhaps too exotic to flourish in a place like Hathersage where the farming interest prevails.

This comment rather suggests that the old domestic system of outworking and the new workshops ran concurrently for the Cooks in the 1820s. After all, the Milwards only built their first mill, next to the *Fountain Inn*, in Redditch in 1838.

The Cooks became part of village life. Robert married twice to sisters Amelia and later Mary White. David married Elizabeth of the long-established Greaves family. The brothers contributed at times to the village Friendly Society, a kind of benefit club,

71 *Barnfield mill chimney, built for steam power in the heyday of Cook and Co.'s manufacture of needles and industrial hackle and gill pins for the textile industry.*

and Robert attended vestry meetings. In 1828 he took on the tenancy of the *Ordnance Arms*, which he held for ten years. Just as the Redditch system operated at the *Fountain Inn*, the *Ordnance Arms* was the place to exchange or pay for rod or coiled wire, or pass half-worked needles on to other craftsmen. Storage in the stables was granted by the owner, Ashton Ashton Shuttleworth, who leased Hall Field to Cook as grazing for his wagon horses between their journeys.

Robert Cook received no enclosures in the 1830 Award but, by the time of the 1832 Land Tax lists, he was occupying a wire mill on Shuttleworth land. This was Barnfield Works, or Cook's, as it was known. In 1833 he was a defendant in a court case as landlord of the *Ordnance Arms*. He was accused by George Morton, a neighbour and also landlord of the *George Inn*, of leaving stinking rubbish in the main street on the site of the old hempyard. The site probably looked and smelt no worse than when it had been a hemp yard long before, although Cook had also acquired some piggeries nearby.

By 1845 he appears as a voter in the Poll Book of 1842-3, living in Barnfield House close to the works. David, his brother, played a smaller part in the business, being the landlord of the *Bell Inn* and also a grocer. He lived at Hillfoot until his death in 1846. Robert Cook's new partner was George Holme Spencer, who continued to be involved even after he established his own factory. Cook's workers staged a 'walk out' just before the Great Exhibition in 1851 but all was well by the time Cook exhibited. Cocker, his competitor, said Cook had the largest works in Hathersage and it certainly appears so on

72 *A needle scourer's bench. Hundreds of unfinished needles were stacked in the wooden trough each day, put in sacking bags with oil and emery powder, and vibrated under a scouring bed to polish them.*

the Ordnance Survey map published in 1893. Robert Cook died in 1866 aged 76, having been in Hathersage for 55 years. Some idea can be gained of his character in the matter of some leases of Roman Catholic property which he had bought and would not sell back. The parish priest, Louis le Dréau, wrote to the Duke of Norfolk's agent, 'Robert Cook is a very strange man to have anything to do with, he growls when one calls on him.' Before his death he relented and returned one land lease without payment. The other leases were sold by his devisees immediately after, ignoring the term of 100 years.

Robert had six children but none of them continued in the family business for in 1873 a public company was formed called Hathersage Works. It was valued at £7,800 when £10 shares in it were being sold. Of the four directors only one Cook name appeared, William Austen Cook of Manchester. Joseph White Broomhead was almost certainly a relation by marriage. William Micklethwaite was from Titanic Steel Works in Sheffield and the Chairman was William Leggoe of Rotherham. In 1880 Cook's old works, now Hathersage Works at Barnfield, was the victim of a 'rattening' incident which was associated with efforts to bring in trade unions. The following report appeared in the *High Peak News* of 11 January 1890:

73 *The 1958 floods where Dale and Hood Brooks meet give some idea of the water power which once moved three waterwheels.*

> Between the hours of twelve and one o'clock on Wednesday at Messrs. Cook and Co., hackle pin manufacturers, Hathersage, some evilly disposed person or persons maliciously placed a

brick between two cog wheels in a shop called the scouring shop. This dastardly deed was discovered as soon as the engine (which is a powerful one) commenced to run, and a loud retort was heard, and on examination it was found the shaft had broken. A similar attempt was made two or three weeks ago in a different part of the mill to do damage to some of the machinery, but fortunately it was found in time. The offender is evidently someone who knows the 'runs' of the works, as not a trace of the act can be brought to reflect upon anyone present. The workmen had all gone home to dinner. The accident has caused a stoppage to part of the works.

Evidently Hathersage Works was still known as Cook's. It is interesting that there was no mention of child or female workers here. By 1900, however, Hathersage Works was no longer in business.

The Cocker Family

On 22 August 1811 the *Sheffield Mercury* carried this advertisement:

> A newly established needle manufactury at Hathersage near Sheffield is carried on by Cocker and Sons, one of whom being brought up in the business and the other being the original cast steel drawer, they flatter themselves that they can supply their friends and the public with not only cheaper but superior articles in the above line than have heretofore been offered. NB Orders from houses of respectability will be met with regular and prompt attention by being addressed to the above in Hathersage.

The Cockers had arrived in Hathersage in the early 18th century, probably from the Manchester area, and Sollomon [*sic*] Cocker's marriage to Elizabeth Windle in 1724 is the first reference to the family in the Hathersage church registers. It was a large family with many branches, some in Sheffield where they had already formed industrial companies and partnerships. These enterprises are worthy of note because at times the Hathersage Cockers would be drawn into them. By 1752 Samuel Cocker and Son were operating the Wheel at Porter Steel Works, Sharrow Vale and, as we have seen, were making steel wire for Benjamin Huntsman. They were still making wire in 1802 for William Huntsman, as was Robert Cocker in Hathersage. Samuel Cocker moved to Porter Steel Works in 1834 and died in 1841. The Cockers acquired Fitzalan Works from 1785 and Nursery Mills from 1855, and these were involved in all aspects of steel processing. The illustration on their letterhead of 1900 puts the continuity of the firm beyond doubt. Having traded under various names, by 1900 they were Cocker Brothers of Sheffield.

In Hathersage, however, Cocker and Sons remained quite a separate firm. The elder Cockers were Thomas (1758-1834) and his brother Jonathan (1763-1827). Their father, Robert (1729-1814), is

234 COCKER & SONS, *Hathersage, Derbyshire*—
Manufacturers.

Needles, in every stage of their manufacture, from the wire of cast steel to the finished article.

The exhibitors, being the drawers of card and other wire, a process which originated with their ancestors, a century ago, Mr. Huntsman, of Attercliffe, who first refined carbonated iron, and which has been a source of great wealth, not only in the manufacture of cast steel, but in the great variety of articles of cutlery for which Sheffield is so celebrated, suggested to them that it would be mutually advantageous if they could succeed in drawing cast steel made from his carbonated iron. The suggestion was adopted, the attempt was made, and the cast steel and the wire made from it are now articles of very extensive exportation.

Specimens numbered in the order of manufacture:—
Wire: 1, cut double length of a needle; 2, straightened; 3, pointed at each end; 4, grooved, for two needles; 5, eyed, for two needles.

Needles: 6, threaded; 7, filed on the sides; 8, filed on the heads; 9, broken in two; 10, drilled in the eye; 11, hardened; 12, tempered; 13, straightened; 14, scoured, first time; 15, scoured, second time; 16, scoured, third time; 17, scoured, fourth time; 18, glazed; 19, headed, and picked from waste; 20, blued in the eye and groove; 21, drilled in the eye; 22, first extra polish; 23, second extra polish; 24, third extra polish; 25, blued in the eye and groove; 26, gold-eyed; 27, papered, twenty-five in a paper; 28, papered and tucked; 29, papered in envelopes; 30, labelled, in envelopes, and on purple paper; 31, in cases.

Wire of various kinds:—32, pinion and click wire, for clocks and watches; 33, music wire, for pianofortes; 34, watch and chronometer spring wire; 35, cast steel, hammered flat, half flat, and square.

Nos. 36-41. Hackles, from large hatchel to 180's fine. Gills, for dividing the fibres of flax in machinery. Hacklepins. Gill-pins. Wool-combers' broaches. Spiral springs.

42. Particles of cast steel, taken from pipes used in conveying away the dust occasioned in grinding needles on dry stones, and which would, if allowed to float in the air, be inhaled by the grinders, thereby causing a complaint until lately very common, and hitherto incurable.

[About twelve or fifteen years ago, several methods were tried to remedy this, but they did not effectually succeed until a powerful fan, as represented in the plan hanging on the boards at the end of the counter, was put up, on which is shown a grinder at work, and the blaze of fire arising from the stone in the act of pointing, with the fan underneath, drawing the dust and particles of steel down the pipe, and leaving the atmosphere of the room perfectly clear and free from all injurious effects; so that dry grinders have now the chance of living as long as other men; without this apparatus they cannot now be induced to work; it is therefore universally adopted.]

74 *The Cocker & Sons of Hathersage entry in the catalogue for the Great Exhibition of 1851.*

THE COCKERS OF HATHERSAGE

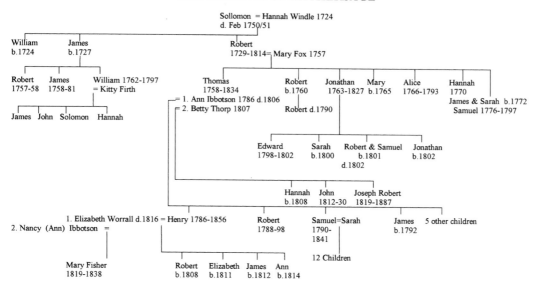

the most shadowy figure of all, appearing in the Hathersage Land Tax lists of 1780 and 1788 as tenant of John Dowel at Carr Head. In the 1801 valuation of local property he was still living at Carr Head in a homestead owned by Thomas Fox, whose daughter he married. The Foxes of the Thorp area were a prominent family in the 16th and 17th centuries. Robert supplied drawn steel wire for William Huntsman in 1802. He died in 1814 aged 84 years.

Thomas Cocker was the most prominent of Robert's sons. He married firstly Ann Ibbotson of Moorseats, one of the many alliances between Cocker and Ibbotson, and secondly Betty Thorpe, and had children by both wives. He was a farmer and landowner as well as a substantial tenant of other landowners. With his younger brother Jonathan he joined the newly formed local Wesleyan group and became a preacher by 1792 and was still preaching in 1824. He was a wealthy man, as his donation of six guineas, one of the highest subscriptions, for the new school of 1804 suggests. He was similarly committed to other charities benefiting Hathersage.

The precise date for the opening of each mill is not known. The Cockers are not listed as owning land until 1818, when Thomas had workshops in the Dale, also leasing the adjoining plot and workshop belonging to the Duke of Devonshire. Formerly the old button mill, his Dale works became known as 'Cockers'. Thomas also owned two plots with tenanted houses and gardens next to the site of the future Atlas Works, which was in business by 1832 when the Land Tax list named Cocker and Sons as tenants of the devisees of the late Ashton Ashton Shuttleworth.

Thomas Cocker had 13 children, although only two sons were associated with his business in Hathersage. Most notable were Henry born in 1786 and Samuel born in 1790. Joseph Robert, born in 1819 to the second marriage, would manage the Atlas Works in the mid-19th century.

Samuel, Thomas's younger son, had a large family. The church register records five of his children christened at one time in 1818. Seven more were to appear on the register up

75 *The early needle pointer had little protection from the metal dust around him before the 1840s.*

to 1834. Samuel held no land but did some wire drawing and farmed with his father. He preached on the same Methodist circuit. By 1822 he was recorded in the register as a needle manufacturer and later as a wire manufacturer. He may have worked at one of the two local Cocker works until his father's death in 1834, when he went to live in Sheffield and work at Porter Works until his death in 1841.

Thomas Cocker's eldest son, Henry Cocker (1786-1856), became the mainstay of Cocker and Sons, Hathersage. He married Ann Ibbotson, born 1792, of Moorseats. In 1818 he was tenant of ten properties but later began to buy his own land. He too was a Methodist preacher in 1824 but by the 1840s had become a churchwarden of St Michael and All Angels parish church, chairing vestry meetings when the proposals for the urgent repairs to the church were being discussed.

Even before 1811 Henry and his family were drawing wire from rod and manufacturing needles, first in barns and other premises and later in the Cocker mill in the Dale with workshops opposite, where the business of making pinion wire, hackle pins and gill pins for combing and carding yarn, fishhooks and needles was increasingly focused. As already noted, Henry may have tried weaving there before that. At some time after 1818 the works, later named Atlas, opened for business just below the confluence of Dale and Hood Brook near the *George Inn* road junction. It is still possible to see the narrow basin on the west bank that housed the water wheel. In 1834, after the death of his father, Henry inherited the business in Hathersage and that is when his brother Samuel went to Sheffield.

Sometime between 1840-41 the Cockers introduced steam power to Dale Mill. At first steam was regarded as an expensive standby when rivers ran dry but later it was accepted as the preferred, dependable, source of power. A three-storey building was erected at Dale Mill, with a boiler house and chimneystack which John Shuttleworth, in a legal action, complained he could see from his house. From the 1830s Henry had borrowed money in two tranches of £600 and £1,500, one of the creditors being David Cooper. In the early 1840s he borrowed another £3,000 which was an early form of mortgage underwritten by the Parker and Shore Bank which itself failed in February 1843.

The bank was established in Sheffield in 1774 and later had a branch in Hathersage. The collapse in 1843 badly affected the finances of Cocker and Sons. The parish church too lost money because of the collapse. Many other banks failed from the 1820s to 1840s because of the inadequacies of the banking system before the reforms of Prime Minister Sir Robert Peel in 1844. Henry Cocker and his son Robert were declared bankrupt by 1847 and Rock House and some of their land, including Dale Mill and its workshops, was sold at auction to repay the debt. They had borrowed a large sum just to convert Dale Mill to steam power and they may have been overcommitted to another project.

76 *The demolition on 24 October 1902 of a works reputed to be Atlas Mill, which closed in May 1902.*

None of these difficulties were apparent three years later in the Great Exhibition of 1851. When Henry Cocker took Atlas Mill products to London, his entry in the catalogue proclaimed the success of his business. In the census of the same year there were separate entries for Henry's workers and those of Joseph Robert Cocker. There were now two works but, with the Dale Mill sold, it is not clear where the second mill was.

A dozen or more craftsmen were needed to produce each needle, and the level of wages was necessarily low when needles were sold at about a shilling a hundred. Parliamentary Enquiries examining poor conditions in mills discovered that particles of metal released into the air during the grinding processes caused lung diseases, drastically shortening the lives of workers. From 1822 various inventions were devised to solve the problem but it was in Hathersage that Henry Cocker found the answer sometime between 1836 and 1839. He invented an extraction fan powered from the main wheel, with 'pipes' or flues that drew the dust outside the mill. The improvement to grinders' health and prolonged life was proudly recorded in the Cocker section of the Great Exhibition catalogue. A coating of rusty dust now covered houses and buildings within eighty yards of Atlas Works and its corrosive qualities damaged window glass and slates, so in response to complaints Cocker extended the pipes into the waters of Hood Brook, a remedy that would earn the wrath of environmentalists today. The system of fan and flues was to be adopted universally, although a similar idea was devised independently in 1845 for needle mills in Redditch.

Henry Cocker died in 1856 aged 75, months after the end of the Crimean War and the same day that Henry Bessamer gave a paper in London announcing his new Steel Converter. By the mid-1860s domestic needles were no longer made in the Atlas Works. The manufacturers in the Redditch area who specialised in needles for domestic, surgical and light textile use now regained pre-eminence. Cockers, renowned for needle making in Britain and Europe for fifty years, continued to exploit the market in steel wire, industrial pins and needles, hackles and gills for textile and other machinery. Fishhooks were made and many other new applications were served: when ladies' crinoline under-hoops became popular in the 1860s, Cockers made the fine steel hoops; wire for the piano and harp was made and so were umbrella ribs and furniture. Samuel Fox of Bradwell, later famous for innovations in umbrella making, was an apprentice to Samuel

Cocker from 1831 to 1834 and followed his master to Sheffield, although he finally set up for himself in Stocksbridge.

It is remarkable that so little is known about the Cocker family bearing in mind its pre-eminence in the village for so many years. The family pedigree in the Jackson Collection has no dates for Henry's children. It refers to Henry Cocker 'of Rock House', which suggests that the pedigree was compiled before 1848 when it was sold, and it records Henry's eldest son as Robert Cocker. Born in 1808, he was working for his father when they were both cited for bankruptcy in 1834. Robert was in New York at the time, but in the Poll Book of 1842 to 1843 he was listed as a voting resident of Hathersage, and he was married by 1844 when his daughter was born. He worked in Sheffield but did not appear in the 1852 Directory, even though his father's business was making spring knives in Pond Street by then. In 1856, however, the year of his father's death, Robert Cocker was wiredrawing under the name Robert Cocker and Co. at Castle Mills in Blonk Street, Sheffield, and by 1860 he was making steel wire goods.

The Cocker pedigree makes no mention of Robert having a family but there is a pencilled reference to his daughter and her 'marriage at the Cathedral, Halifax, Nova Scotia on 3 October 1867; Robert Henry Clive of Birmingham to Mary Fisher Cocker only child of the late Robert Cocker of Sheffield'. Official references in the archives in Nova Scotia confirm that Mary's mother was also called Mary and that her father's occupation was wire merchant. There is no reference to Robert Cocker's death in the Hathersage or General Register Office records, nor does he appear in Sheffield or Hathersage cemetery records. He was alive in 1860 when the Directory of that year for Sheffield refers to occupation and private address. It seems likely that he died in North America some time between 1860 and 1867.

Joseph Robert Cocker, Henry's half-brother born in 1819, was working in tandem with Henry in 1851 but with separate workforces. At Henry's death Joseph Robert took his place and was still running Atlas Works in 1868. The business had begun to decline by the 1880s, as the local cotton industry, succumbing to imperial competition and the mass production of competitors, no longer needed its output. After Joseph Robert's death in 1887 his son John, once a traveller for the firm, inherited. He had lived at home and in 1887 married his mother's former maid, Harriet. Within a year he was dead. Harriet married a Wesleyan Superintendent, and the Cockers ceased to occupy the site. Atlas closed for five years, and after a short revival it closed for good in 1902. Five years later it was demolished. The other four mills in the village were adapted to other uses.

77 *The advertisement for Tobias Child & Co. in* White's Sheffield Directory *of 1868.*

David Cooper

David Cooper's family had lived as landowners in Padley from at least the 17th century. Cooper was a quarry owner and millstone maker and, by 1840, the landlord of the *Scotsmans' Pack Inn*. He appeared in the Hathersage census of 1841 and directories thereafter as a manufacturer of needles and hackle and gill pins and cast steel wire. From the Cammell Papers we learn that he was one of Henry Cocker's creditors when Cocker borrowed money in the 1830s. Cooper bought Dale Mill and other property at the Cocker sale of 1848. It seems more than likely that he used the Dale Mill site, with its wheels and machinery already in place, for his needle making.

Tobias Child and James Marsden

Tobias Child was another incomer who arrived earlier than is sometimes thought. Born in 1806, he was a witness of Thomas Cocker's will of 1829, the year that Child was married to Martha Furniss. In 1831 their son Edward was born. In 1832 he paid Land Tax as joint owner with James Marsden of a farm, where Thomas Marsden, once the village schoolteacher, was tenant. Originally from Darlington, a region of iron and steel production, Tobias became a manufacturer of steel wire, hackle and gill pins in Hathersage. As a tenant of John Spencer Ashton Shuttleworth, old Ashton's young son, Tobias Child was open for business by 1841 in the former Pearson Workshops later renamed Victoria Works in honour of the Queen. He employed 15 workers at first, the number rising to 28 later, in the long two-storeyed workshop visible today, the only building left of the mill complex in Mill Lane. His mill was situated on Hood Brook, downstream from Cocker's Altas Works and Cook's Works at Barnfield, and Child continued to use waterpower long after his rivals had turned to steam. He also leased the *Ordnance Arms* after Robert Cook gave up the tenancy, probably using it for the same purpose, but lived at Furniss House (now called Hawthorndene). The census of 1881 shows he was still living at Furniss House where he died in 1883.

In the early days, one of Martha Child's nephews, James Marsden, lived with the family at Furniss House. He was born in 1833 and in the census of 1861 was living with the Childs while travelling for the business. Later he was to live next door with his wife and children, the eldest son being named Tobias. In 1871 he declared he was a 'pin maker' in the census. Marsden's pins were hackle and gill pins and, as Tobias Child became older, James Marsden and his stepson ran Victoria Works. Eventually in the 1880s John Stead took over in order to make gramophone needles and steel pins. Steam power must have been adopted at some time for the boiler blew up in 1910 and the mill fell into disuse. John Stead's son, writing in 1932 from his Manor Works in Sheffield, described how in the late 19th century German machines were introduced to make needles in Hathersage. He remembered the wire mill at Ringinglow that had supplied them, and he saw its chimney being demolished after the First World War.

78 *Steel needles being tempered at high temperatures and quenched in water, as part of the hardening process.*

Ralph Greaves and John Darvill

The most prominent 'Top Mill' on the main street has the most perplexing past. Known as 'Darvill's Mill' by some, John Darvill neither established it nor owned it. Originally Ralph Greaves of a Moscar family occupied a workshop on or near the site. The course of the main street has been altered over time and Greaves workshop, being water-powered, may have been closer to Dale Brook near Thimble Hall. Greaves was an early wire and needle manufacturer and in 1832 was a tenant leasing a house and mill from Ashton Ashton Shuttleworth's devisees. He was described in the parish registers as a manufacturer but in a directory of 1845 he is listed as a 'gentleman', and after that time no other occupation is listed for him. He took part in vestry meetings for a time and one of his daughters, Elizabeth, married David Cook of the Barnfield connection. After 1849 Greaves' name disappeared from records.

It was after Greaves' time that John Darvill had connections with this workshop. Although he had come from Alcester and his wife from Redditch, he had been in the village for some years. His name is first associated with needle making at 'Darvill' or Top Mill nearly forty years after the Cooks' arrival from the Redditch area and just before the Great Exhibition in 1851. He is not listed as a manufacturer in directories and entries in parish registers refer to him as a needle stamper or needle maker. Before long he had turned to other occupations and was a shopkeeper in 1856 and later a hackle pin traveller and a highway surveyor. His son William lodged for a time with Charles Rastall, a needle pointer from Redditch. William was a needle scourer in 1871 and a hackle pin hardener and temperer in 1881; he might have worked at the Top Mill. It is just possible that the Cockers leased Top Mill, wherever sited, and the large sum of money they borrowed was for its rebuilding and adaptation to steam power. It might be where a second group of workers was employed in the census of 1851 with Darvill in charge. The metal business at Darvill Mill closed in the 1880s and is not shown on the Ordnance Survey map of 1883. By 1899 the building had been turned to other uses, J. Armfield's grocer's shop facing the main street. Darvill himself died in 1898, long after the heyday of the local needle industries.

Summary

Wire and needle manufacture in Hathersage was not restricted to three or four employers, and there were in the village families with needle skills like the Rastalls, Richmonds and Darvills who came from Redditch attracted by the demand for skilled needle workers. The demise of the needle industry in Hathersage was due to its size. In 1868 there were four main workshops, which could not match the Redditch trade where 117 firms made cheaper needles using cheap coal and canal transport and merged to form larger companies. The railway came to Redditch in 1859 and Studley in 1868 while Hathersage mills were all but extinct when the railway arrived in 1894.

Chapter 29

The Transformation of Hathersage

When the first national census was taken in 1801 there were 498 people in Hathersage and its hamlets. Comparison with later census statistics can only be approximate given that the boundaries varied at different dates and enumeration rules changed, but by 1851 the population had doubled to 1,030 for Hathersage and Outseats and it was 1,241 in the 1861 census. A small decline was noted in 1871 and 1881, rising again in 1891 to 1,210. Today it numbers about 2,000.

Families had moved into Hathersage from Hill hamlet and outlying areas in the 19th century leaving Geer Green School deserted. The new subscription school, opened in 1804 in the main street, eventually became too full even though not all parents could afford the fee of a few pence a week. Early Factory Acts controlling working hours for children applied only to textile mills and certain other industries but the minimum age for the few local children working in needle mills was never lower than eight. Only in 1867 did an Extension Act redefine workshops and protect more children. The precision needed for needle making did not lend itself to child labour, although Thomas Schofield at age 11 claimed to be a wire scourer and his sister, aged 13, a packager. The census of 1851 is not entirely clear but suggests that about 25 children worked in mills, with 174 children staying at home and 150 attending school. It put 244 people in the needle mills and 144 in agriculture from a population of 1,030. A few women were employed making umbrella ribs and Widow Higginbottom in 1861 was a needle hammerer. Two Friendly Societies had been in existence locally since the 18th century to enable members to save and receive succour in time of trouble.

At times there was unrest in the village which reflected the issues current in Sheffield, whether corn prices, the 1832 Reform Bill, or trade unionism. The counties were unaffected by the Metropolitan Police Act of 1829 so the parish constable was left to keep order with his horn, handcuffs and staff but without the aid of the old curfew, a distant memory by 1825. His ultimate sanction was the lock-up. This had been located

79 The Catholic Chapel, built in 1806. The presbytery was built soon after.

80 *The Hearse House, built in 1821, was already a ruin when a tree destroyed it in 1938.*

in different places including, at times, the constable's house, but in 1826 the Duke of Devonshire announced that he would pay for a new cell. After much debate about its site and construction it was built adjacent to the Hearse House in 1828. The role of the constable was only abolished in 1856 when county police forces became compulsory.

The new subscription school appeared in 1804 on the main street where three farmhouses once stood alone in their fields. It is now the parish room but the subscription board is still there. The new Catholic Chapel was completed by 1806, the presbytery and bell tower later additions. The Methodist Chapel was built in 1807 but obscured by a new façade of 1872 until it was demolished in 1939 to make way for the existing chapel. Close by is the weathered notice of its 1815 Sunday school, visible only from a private garden. The *Ordnance Arms* was built in 1808 in expectation of the 1811 branch turnpike. The Hearse House, which stored the new 1821 hearse when not in use, stood near today's bus shelter. It fell into disrepair long before it was demolished in the exceptional October gales of 1938 by a falling tree. A dame school once used the upper room and vestry meetings were held there for a time.

The main road saw more changes. Downing Terrace, named after its builder, was built on Catholic land in 1834. Hathersage Hall, at the top of the village street, was damaged by fire in November 1841 and its new frontage built soon after. The Hall's stables were dressed in similar stonework, that is also echoed in the building style of Top Mill nearby. By now two needle mills using steam power were working in the main street.

81 *The Hearse House would store a hearse similar to this one.*

82 *Hall Farm was refurbished when the Hall underwent some rebuilding after being damaged by a fire in 1841.*

The gentry built new residences. James Holworthy had created Brookfield Hall and estate in the mid-1820s from a farm and some cottages half a mile from the village. At the confluence of Hood Brook with the River Derwent, Nether Hall was built for John S.A. Shuttleworth in 1841 and, over the years, the new houses of the mill owners appeared: Rock House, Moorseats, Bell Vue, Barnsfield House and Furniss House. Vicar Nussey, who vainly proposed marriage to Charlotte Brontë, enlarged the vicarage for another bride.

The clergy of each church taught scripture and faith to illiterate children in Sunday schools, giving momentum to the progression towards day schools. Father George Jinks, priest from 1824-33, opened a Sunday school in 1825 in a stone building adjoining the Catholic Chapel. Subsequently he used the room as a public library for the whole village and his successor turned the library into a day school for Catholics in 1846 that was to expand in 1864 and not for the last time.

The Rev. Henry Collingham had been vicar of St Michael's parish church since 1847 and drove forward the building of St Michael's Church of England School in 1858. The project had been delayed in the 1840s by Vicar Le Cornu's declining health and the short three-year tenure of his successor, Henry Nussey, and Collingham himself had first to oversee the repair of Hathersage church and the building of Bamford church in the next parish. By 1858 the vicar and his committee of parishioners were ready to start building the new school and the foundation stone was finally laid in June. The cost

83 *Brookfield Hall in 1868, with the changes which James Holworthy had made in 1825.*

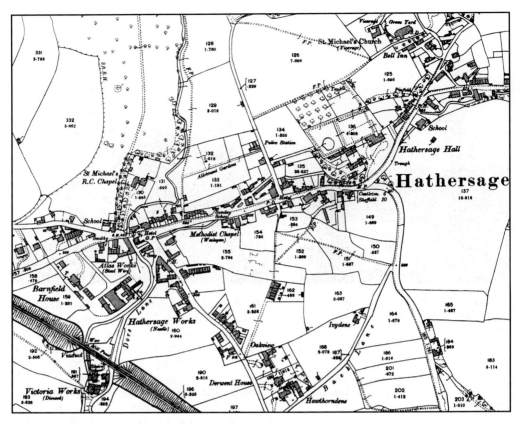

84 *Hathersage on the 1898 Ordnance Survey map.*

was just over £900, a large grant of £300 being given by the Council of Education and £30 by the Anglican National Society. It is said that Thomas Eyre of Moorseats, having purchased the land from the Duke of Devonshire, gave the site for the school, but this is questionable since the accounts show £150 as the cost of the site. The grand opening on New Year's Eve 1858, with the building lit by candelabras, lasted for hours. The school was decorated with banners celebrating its greatest benefactors. After the dedication service, when the vicar made an impressive sermon and very long prayer, there was tea and entertainment by the pupils.

The *Derbyshire Courier* of 1 January 1859 gives as much insight into social attitudes as it does into the event. It spoke of the need for 'the extension of education among the poorer classes ... in secluded villages where progress of intelligence has been retarded by the scantiness and poverty of the people'. In fact, Hathersage had already subscribed for earlier schools, the church and chapels.

All ages were taught and in 1893 an Evening Continuation School met at what were soon to be called the New Schools. During the 36-year headship of Mr Noah Roden one tradition continued 'according to custom', the children being dismissed by the Pancake Bell mid-morning Shrove Tuesday for a half-day holiday. Evening class for boys began in the First World War. After the Second World War one of the last rural adult evening institutes was held and by day a craft centre became available for the over-13 age group. The Centenary Year in 1958 was celebrated with a pageant on Seel Field

85 *St Michael and All Angels Church and vicarage, where Charlotte Brontë stayed.*

86 *The interior of Hathersage parish church before its restoration by Butterfield in 1851.*

devised by the headmaster Harry Schofield in his last year of office. Under Mr Tom Meehan, headmaster from 1959–82, the school acquired more amenities and additions to become the pleasant site of today.

In 1894 the railway to link Sheffield and Manchester was opened giving Hathersage people easier contact with the outside world. The Padley Tunnel, the longest hill tunnel at the time, began at Padley Station close to the ruins of Padley Hall. It was to be costly in terms of human lives. From 1889–94, 29 men died, four killed outright, two in the tunnel. Five women and three children died in their makeshift huts in Padley Woods and Hathersage and 18 infants of two and under also lost their lives. The vicar recording the deaths in the burial register added the word 'navvie' to each of the 58 entries. Accidents, poor living conditions, the high infant mortality of the period and outbreaks of smallpox and diphtheria all played a part and it is unlikely that the services of the village vaccinator or the temporary fever hospital in 1893 above Booths could help these poor families.

Censuses and directories give a picture of a self-sufficient village, with tailors, bootmakers, dressmakers, drapers and corn dealers. By 1894 a doctor and surgeon were in residence. A bank had opened and the Conservative Party had a local agent. Inns and beer houses abounded to quench the thirst of the declining number of quarry workers or the increasing needs of tourists, while *The Butcher's Arms*, now *The Little John*, offered accommodation to cyclists.

Chapter 30

The Vestry Years

The controlling group of people in any parish in the 19th century was the Vestry Meeting, which regulated the finances and affairs of church and community. In some areas it met once a year near Easter, to agree poor rates, select committees and elect parish officers, although in Hathersage it met more often. It was a 'closed' vestry where a select few nominated or co-opted each other. The names of old families and the metal manufacturers appear as churchwardens or vestry members. The Shuttleworth squires often chaired meetings and all the mill owners were involved at times. The scope of the Vestry's work ranged from small items, like bell rope repair, fox elimination, paying for a vagrant's medicine or repair of the pinfold, to major issues like the new valuation of property for the Church Rate in the late 1830s when members advertised for a professional land valuer to deal with such a sensitive task.

One great problem facing the Vestry was the 'very decayed' state of the parish church. The vicar, John Le Cornu, had held the living for over fifty years and resisted change in his last years. After his death in 1844, the Vestry had to decide whether to make essential repairs or carry out more extensive renovation. It was decided to invite William

87 *Job Mottram of Lower Booths.*

Butterfield to undertake a full survey and in March 1849 his plans were adopted, tenders were put out and the Church Rate increased to 3d. in the pound to meet some of the cost. There was a great public response and the Duke of Devonshire, J.S.A. Shuttleworth, and Hannah Wright, James Holworthy's sister-in-law and heir to his estate, gave £100 each. By 1852 there was a grand opening of the refurbished church.

This was to be the heyday of the Vestry and by the late 1850s less business was recorded in the minutes as matters were withdrawn from its jurisdiction by statute. The old Overseers of the Poor now answered to the Bakewell Union, which had taken over Vestry responsibilities and by 1868 church rates were abolished. The Vestry began to meet annually to discuss purely church matters. By 1878 parishioners were included in the election of churchwardens and attended what developed into the annual Parish Meeting. In 1880 Hathersage objected, without success, to being included in the Bakewell Highway District.

By the 1890s new names appearing in Vestry records include the Rev. Cutler, George Cammell of steel and ship-building fame, who had bought the Brookfield estate, the new headmaster Noah Roden, Job Mottram, Joseph Crossland and William Bocking, who was the rate collector for Bakewell Union but elected by the Vestry. In 1894 the new Local Government Act established a three-tier system of local government with the secular Parish Council as the lowest tier under District and County control. The effective change took place by the simple expedient of many of the old Vestry leaders being elected to the new Parish Council. They were often the major ratepayers with a wealth of experience in village politics. In the early years of the 20th century outstanding business from Vestry days was occasionally referred to the council meeting and in 1909 it was called upon to consider the Lighting and Watching Act of 1833.

Within a year of its being set up, the Parish Council and the church Parish Meeting asked the trustees of the two charity schools of 1718 and 1804 to sell the schools to the Parish Council. This was an intricate matter involving the Charity Commissioners, who finally gave permission. The valuation for the schools was £48 and in March 1897 the sale was completed. With public funds strictly allocated, it was the vicar, Rev. Cutler, who raised over £47 by holding jumble sales and other entertainments, and so the Marsden 1804 school became the Parish Room which was to have many uses during the 20th century.

Chapter 31

The Running Tide

When Queen Victoria died in January 1901, the Boer War still continued, the new Labour Party had not yet made its mark and the Liberal reforms of 1906 had yet to add security to people's lives. Working conditions were still harsh and the threat of the workhouse to the poor and elderly was very real. There were, however, fleeting glimpses of progress and moments of leisure that led to the expectation of a better future.

The Longshaw Sheepdog Trials

Events on the old parish boundaries were to attract attention in the early years of Edward VII's reign. On the eastern boundary the Longshaw Sheep Dog Trials had begun. Reputed to have started as a contest between a gamekeeper and a shepherd, the first Trial was planned for a day in March 1898 but was cut short by a blizzard. The competition continued the next day on a less exposed field. Another Trial was held in September 1898 and thereafter it became an annual event except in war years. There has been increasing diversity of competition to show the skills of sheep dog and master on courses with arranged obstacles. The committee of the Longshaw Sheep Dog Trials Association was composed from early days of farmers and elders of the district under the patronage of the Cavendish family. The nearby *Fox House Inn* provided the annual hotpot feast and the singsong for this male-dominated society.

In the 20th century the trials attracted participants from all over the country and in 1946 an American took part. Attendance rose to many thousands over the now three-day meetings. Buses used to run from Sheffield every ten minutes. The events were broadcast in 1945 and appeared on newsreels at times and in 1950 there were 20,000 spectators. From the beginning the Association funded local hospital beds and even after the National Health Service began in 1947 it continued to support medical charities. The rules

88 *A Longshaw Sheepdog Trial.*

89 *Coronation celebrations for Edward VII in August 1902, where Back Lane meets the Sheffield Road (in foreground).*

are sacrosanct and even spectators must conform. There must be no clapping during events that might prevent the working dogs from hearing their masters' whistles. Sheepdogs who have been shown at Longshaw have very occasionally become film stars in their own right: Pal Glen featured in *Song of the Plough* in 1934 and Fleet became 'Lassie' after the Second World War.

Today the Trials have supporting attractions showing or selling rural goods. There are many silver cups or trophies for each competition and there is pride in the Association's standards and its ability to provide new tasks for competitors. In the last ten years, the Association has had its first lady Secretary, Sheila Humphreys, a member of a local farming family.

The Dams

While the village celebrated the accession of Edward VII in 1901 plans were far advanced to create two reservoirs along the valley of the River Derwent to provide water for the Midlands towns of Nottingham, Leicester and Derby. The area affected was the north-west river boundary of the old parish of Hathersage, where Abbey Brook flowed into the Derwent.

A temporary new village was born when an army of workers and engineers settled on the slopes by Birchinlee Farm. Birchinlee, or Tin Town as it became known, was a collection of single-storey houses, a school, a hospital and a 'rec' or hall for social events.

90 *Birchinlee, the temporary village built to house the dam workers.*

91 *Dr Lander, the physician in the Hope Valley who attended at Birchinlee in its first few months.*

Sports and celebrations were held on the fields of Abbey Brook Farm. In the first winter months, Dr Graham Lander, the Hathersage doctor, would make the 20-mile round trip on horseback or by trap to attend to patients there. A disagreement over what, in reality, was a modest request for a higher fee led the Derwent Valley Water Board to bring in its own medical officers. A railway was built as far as Bamford to carry materials for the reservoirs and dams and two carriages were added for passengers. It was also used by young people from Hathersage and Bamford to travel to the Saturday night dances at the Birchinlee rec.

The waters began to build up after Howden Dam was completed in 1912 and Derwent Dam in 1916. By now Birchinlee and its railway had been dismantled and the occupants had begun to move on to new projects. Derwent Dam was two miles from Derwent village, which had only four years' respite before the threat of more dams affected its future. In 1920 an Act was passed giving the DVWB new powers to create dams on the rivers Derwent and Ashop. In the event only one big one was built. Ladybower Dam was completed in 1945 when King George VI opened the control towers and the waters began to cascade. Mighty pipes carrying the reservoir water run southward through Hathersage on their journey to the Midlands. Ashopton and Derwent village, the old berewick of Hathersage, were demolished in 1943 and the graves removed to other churchyards. The 17th-century Derwent Hall of the Balguy family and the church, only built in 1868, were dismantled. The spire survived for a few years and could be seen above the waters but it was destroyed in 1947 as it attracted intrepid tourists to approach it in times of drought.

The War Memorial for Derwent and Woodland overlooks the tranquil waters of the reservoirs. It is an outstandingly beautiful scene and the medieval sparrow hawks of King John would still recognise their habitat. The only discordant note would be RAF 617 Squadron making practice runs in 1944 over the Derwent and Howden reservoirs in preparation for the real Dambuster attack on the German dams which they resembled. The bouncing bombs themselves were tested on the Norfolk coast where they could be retrieved as they bounced on the beach.

Utilities

In the lively village of Hathersage it was not always easy for the new local governing bodies to work together. The Rural District Council would only show the sewerage plans to the Parish Council after repeated requests. The early Parish Council was torn between keenness to control amenities like refuse collection and the need to stay within its precept, the rate being set at a maximum of 3d. in the pound by an Act of 1894. There have been many attempts since the 1930s to unite Outseats and Hathersage Parish Councils, the last being in 1981.

In 1898 an electrical company approached the Parish Council with an offer to instal street lighting, which was refused. The vicar in 1900 offered to instal at his own expense

92 *Howden Dam in its opening year of 1912.*

a street lamp at the steep footpath on the south side of the churchyard, but it was only in 1908 that the Parish Council accepted a gas supply in the parish. The Hathersage Gas Company came into existence and a gasworks and holder were built; an entry in the school records in 1909 remarks how much it was needed in the classroom where it was too dark to read or sew on a December afternoon. Domestic use of gas came after the First World War when a few street lamps were to be lit at set times and, as recorded in 1924, 'even during moonlight'.

By 1930 the Parish Council was enquiring about an electrical supply, but it was not until 1937 that a demonstration light was installed in Mill Lane, close to the new council houses. It was retained but, even so, a new gaslight was bought for Sheffield Road. The battle for lighting was made irrelevant when the Second World War brought blackout to the village. After 1943 some lighting was restored and, by 1946, 46 gas lamps existed. Electric lighting was only installed in 1961.

In spite of the great dams, which provided water to remote towns elsewhere, Hathersage had to wait 14 years for all of its inhabitants to receive piped water. An early reservoir in the Dale and the water from Greens House served some homes. In the late 1920s

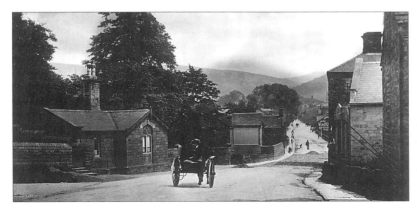

93 *Main Street before 1902, with Atlas Mill, the Catholic school and the George Inn in view.*

94 *Gothic Row in the early 20th century before modern council houses replaced its cottages.*

many public meetings were held to explore other sources of water for Sheffield Road and the village at large. Indignant householders like Mr Scorah spoke feelingly of having to walk across others' land to use a neighbour's well. Another resident had to boil all the water taken from his trough. The covered reservoir above Booths solved the problem, although to this day some outlying properties have spring water privately piped.

The effort to obtain piped water was assisted by the pressure to have a local fire brigade. When the idea was first mooted in 1906 the Parish Council declared it was beyond its jurisdiction. It declined a joint action with Outseats to acquire a fire engine in 1926 and by 1932 was asking Sheffield Fire Brigade about its charges for attendance. Finally, in 1933, fire equipment was bought and stored in the Parish Room and later in a Nissen hut. Brigade members were recruited and paid two shillings for attending each of the six drills a year. It would be 1962 before the present Fire Station was opened in Oddfellows Road.

The First World War

As families moved to Sheffield to work in munitions factories, or men joined the services, school numbers began to fall. In March 1916 B Company of the Yorks and Lancs Regiment used the school as a bivouac one night. Dr Lander headed a committee to administer a Local Distress Fund and another centralising committee, including four women, was set up to coordinate the work of local governing bodies in an emergency.

When Tin Town was dismantled in 1914, many of its huts, the bathhouse and the rec hall were sent to Wakefield to prepare for a prisoner-of-war camp, but the beds and bedding were given to the military Auxiliary Hospital opened in Hathersage in the Wesleyan Institute, itself recently built in 1907. This was run by the Red Cross VAD Unit 38 and had about thirty beds for soldiers convalescing from their wounds. At first used for Belgian soldiers, later patients included British, Commonwealth and Anzac troops, and by the end of the war two to three hundred patients a year had passed through.

95 *Gas Holders at Hathersage Gas Works until 1986.*

96 *Cottages c.1925 on the hillside below the Millstone Inn. They have now been demolished.*

The minutes of the Parish Council from 1909-24 are missing and there is silence as to why there was no public war memorial as in most other villages (although there is a memorial in the parish church and another in the grounds of the Catholic Chapel). When Mrs Dorothy Shuttleworth attended the opening of the Memorial Hall on 9 October 1929 she divided her bouquet and laid flowers at each memorial. By 1925 a Memorial Hall was planned. Originally meant to be on the main road near the Hearse House, it was eventually built in Oddfellows Road, incorporating the old Primitive Methodist Church. In its 76 years of existence it has seen many social occasions including, in earlier days, dances and film shows.

Amenities

The Playing Field on Back Lane was once administered by the Hathersage Welfare Association but by 1928 it wanted to pass the task to a reluctant Parish Council. The

97 *An aerial view of Hathersage, c.1930-4.*

98 *The opening of the new Methodist Chapel, 30 December 1939. George Lawrence and wife are front left. Third from right in the back row is Alfred Stead, whose family made gramophone needles at Victoria Mill in the 1900s. He was MD of Manor Works in Sheffield in 1939.*

99 *Ladybower Reservoir was opened by King George VI in September 1945. The gates give access to the valve house and dam walls. In the distance is the Ashopton viaduct on the Sheffield to Glossop route. Close to it lies the submerged village of Ashopton.*

Council was persuaded in March 1934 to take on the burden and to hold the site in perpetuity as a public playing field, having been helped by the gift of the freehold from Major Shuttleworth for the purpose. During the Silver Jubilee of King George V in 1935 trees were planted there by children in the King's honour. A few months later, when the King died, there were plans to give the field memorial gates and name it 'King George V's Memorial Field'. At first it created problems. The noise of children playing on the swings led to the swings being chained on Sundays and a neighbour had to be deterred from throwing rubbish over the wall. In 1938 the field became one of the King George V's Fields after the Foundation gave a grant of £50 to the Parish Council.

During the 1930s Mr and Mrs G.H. Lawrence, residents of Hathersage, became benefactors to the village, planning and funding leisure areas near the Memorial Hall. A successful Sheffield manufacturer of razors, George Lawrence was responsible for the Bowling Green that opened in 1934 to replace an earlier one at the *George Inn*. A pleasance was added and a swimming pool in 1936. The tennis courts were also part of the complex. When a Methodist Chapel was planned Mr Lawrence offered £5,000 to help the building fund and his wife paid for a new organ. The chapel opened in December 1939.

The Second World War

At the beginning of the war in September 1939, George Lawrence presented a firefighting trailer to add to the resources of the village fire fighters. A year later this village benefactor was killed at his Laurel Works in the Sheffield blitz of 13 December 1940.

Preparations had been made nationally even before the war. In Hathersage the ARP was formed and the LDV became the Home Guard which, in the early days of the war, was to train pigeons as message carriers. Some of its soldiers were given gelignite to blow bridges if there was a German invasion. In May 1940, an anti-aircraft unit of the regular army, 283 Field Battery, 123 Field Regiment, Royal Artillery arrived. The soldiers were billeted all round the village, their vehicles and guns parked on the field where Moorland Road is now.

During their stay of two months the village also received the soldiers returning from Dunkirk who were transferred from Channel ports to places all over Britain to recover from their ordeal. Hathersage received 80 of the many troops sent to the Hope Valley and the village was stretched to house them; certainly some were accommodated in what is now The *Little John Hotel* until they returned to active duty.

The War Office commandeered the facilities of the Lawrence complex, the swimming pool, green and tennis courts until mid-1940. The tearoom was retained for a time but, later in the war, it was used for school meals, although they were eaten in the Lawrence Room in the Memorial Hall which was intended as an evacuation dispersal centre for children. Another military presence was a search light unit encamped near North Lees.

Blackout brought the need to paint pavement curbs white and petrol was severely restricted for private cars and many were laid up for the war. The Dig for Victory campaign persuaded people to grow their own vegetables and the football and cricket pitches were used for allotments despite the intrusion of stray sheep. Some bombs fell close to the Dale Road but a few miles away the unfinished Ladybower Dam led a charmed life. Before the end of the war, some street lighting reappeared and village optimism revealed itself in 1943 with a one-day swimming gala and the first Hathersage Show. It would be two years before peace was declared when the siren, bought by subscription, could be sold and more names were added to the memorials.

Chapter 32

Modern Times

In 1945 getting back to normal was uppermost in people's minds, but the world had moved on. By 1947 there was a very real fear that another war would break out over the future of Berlin. The worst winter in living memory trapped the village in snow. Food rationing got tighter. It is no wonder that people looked for happier pursuits. In the past these had been led by a few, as at the Longshaw Trials and in the days of the Lawrence philanthropy; now there was a general wish to take part in organising activities. The last attempt at masterminding leisure was the launch of the Ex-Servicemen's clubs in 1946 to support local sport and social meetings. Under a church initiative drama groups were formed, like the St Michael's Players in Hathersage.

Public expectation began to change. The Summer Celebrations, in existence by 1950, were more in tune with the times than the old Wakes Week and Michaelmas Fair which ceased after 1953. The Celebrations in turn were replaced by the Hathersage Gala in 1958, organised by the school PTA until 1971. Nowadays the Gala's own committee produces the annual week-long event and throughout the year committees of the many other societies and sports clubs in Hathersage work hard to satisfy their members' interests and energies.

The old parish of Hathersage has lost ground since the destruction of Derwent village in 1943 and the merging of the two Padleys into the parish of Grindleford in 1987. Outseats township of the 17th century has become a civil parish since the 1894

100 *David Mellor's award-winning Round Building which transformed the Gas Works site after 1986.*

101 *A parade of floats in Gala Week in the 1960s. The* Ordnance Arms *was renamed the* Hathersage Inn *in 1964.*

Act, and in the early days Hathersage Parish Council yielded land to it. Hathersage is now in the Peak District National Park created in 1951.

The village has grown, with its pre- and post-war council houses and suburb famously dubbed Shanty Town. The old gasworks has gone and David Mellor's award-winning Round Building takes its place. The trains are more numerous and the shops are fewer. The Post Office moved for a third time in a hundred years to its present site in 1961. The beerhouses and taverns that quenched the thirsts of farmers, needlemakers and quarrymen are a distant memory. A few inns remain, each with a new image but a historic past: the *George*, so long the venue of court barons and inquests; the *Scotsmans' Pack* serving the carriers on the old turnpike and the *Millstone* the quarrymen from the Edges; the *Plough* once the site of a smelting operation, and the *Little John*, under one of its earlier names, receiving the weary Dunkirk troops to sleep where they might. Church and chapels now combine, their ecumenical efforts highlighted at the popular outdoor Christmas Crib Service in the middle of the village. The Millennium Garden above the main street provides a welcome pause. Two of the needle mills, which belched smoke for nearly half a century in the days of steam power, are now apartment blocks. The village is in many ways a dormitory of Sheffield but it draws many visitors, walkers, climbers and photographers. Its scenery has been used in films like the *Princess Bride* and a new *Pride and Prejudice*. Hang gliders float over Bronze-Age fields and walkers pass Padley Hall where Catholic priests were seized to go to Tudor martyrdom.

On winter evenings the hills close in on the village street, brave with its shop lights. People point out the old barn on Dog Kennel slopes which, in childhood, they imagined was a castle and where the sledging was good in winter. The farmer arriving at a local shop on his tractor may well bear the name of an ancestor we have met in the 17th century. If not, he is certainly related to someone in the family tree. The acts

102 *The path to the village street ran past this rural scene until the 1990s.*

of kindness remembered from past times of trouble are still there when a neighbour gardens for an old resident or groups fund-raise on a grand scale for good causes to help those less fortunate.

Pescatani, Romans, Danes, distant lords of the manor, Hanoverian military families and Victorian needlemakers have all passed through and some have stayed. Like them, we are all incomers at sometime but we now carry the mantle of care for the future of the village.

Bibliography

Abbreviations for references
  BPDLMHS – *Bulletin of the Peak District Lead Mines Historical Society*
  CRS – Catholic Record Society
  DAJ – *Journal of Derbyshire Archaeological Society*
  DANHJ – *Derbyshire Archaeological and Natural History Journal*
  DAS – Derbyshire Archaeological Society
  DRO – Derbyshire Record Office (Matlock)
  DRSS – Derbyshire Record Society Series
  EHR – *English Historical Review*
  IAR – *Industrial Archaeological Review*
  NH – *Northern History*
  PRO – Public Record Office now The National Archives
  THAS – *Transactions of the Hunter Archaeological Society*

Addy, S.O., 'Little John's Grave and the Lawful Village Perch', *DAJ* vol. 46 (1924-5)
Aikin, J., *A Description of the Countryside round Manchester* (1795)
Anderson, J.J., *Roman Derbyshire* (1985)
Ashmore, O., *The Early Textile Industry in the Derwent Valley*, Derbyshire Miscellany (1957)
Austin, M.R., 'Religion and Society in Derbyshire during the Industrial Revolution', *DAJ* vol. 93 (1973)
Bagshawe Collection: Sheffield Archives
Barnatt, J. and Smith, K., *The Peak District, Landscapes through Time* (2004)
Barnatt, J., 'Bronze Age Remains on the East Moors of the Peak', *DAJ* vol. 106-7 (1986-7)
Beckett, J.V., *The East Midlands from A.D. 1000* (1988)
Bellamy, J.G., 'The Coterel Gang, an Anatomy of a Band of Criminals in the 14th Century', *EHR* vol. 179 (1964)
Beresford, M. and Hurst, J. (ed.), *Deserted Villages* (1971)
Bishops of Coventry, Bishops' Transcripts, Lichfield Joint Record Office
Blanchard, I.S.W., *Duchy of Lancaster: Cases in the Duchy Council 1485-1580*, DAS Record Series (1971)
Blanchard, I.S.W., 'Derbyshire Lead Production 1195-1505', *DAJ* vol. 91 (1971)
Bowles, C., 'History of Abney', *DAJ* vol.29 (1907)
Branigan, K. (ed.), *Rome and the Brigantes* (1980)
Brighton, J.T., *The Gell Family in the 16th and 17th Centuries* (1980)
Brighton, J.T., *Sir John Gell and the Civil Wars in Derbyshire* (1981)
Brighton, J.T., *Royalist and Roundheads in Derbyshire* (1981)
Brighton, Trevor, *The Discovery of the Peak District: From Hades to Elysium* (2004)
Brooksbank, J.H., *The Story of Hathersage* (1932)
Brooksbank, J.H., 'The History of Castleton', *THAS* vol. 3 (1925)

Burton, I.E., *The Royal Forest of the Peak* (1966)

Calendar of Patent Rolls of Henry IV 1405-8, vol. 3 PRO

Calendars of Inquisitions Post Mortem, Edward III, Henry VII, HMSO (1955) and Henry VIII, HMSO (1960)

Cammell Deeds, Sheffield Archives

Carrington, W.A., 'A Subsidy List of the Hundred of Scarsdale 1599', *DAJ* vol. 24 (1902)

Cecil Papers, Derbyshire Recusancy Lists 1592-3 Miscellanea, CRS 1916, 1921

Chapman, S.D., *The Cotton Industry in the Industrial Revolution* (1972)

Charity Commission, Further Report concerning Charities of Derbyshire (1827)

Chatsworth Papers, Hardwick Drawer, and selected boxes

Clark, R., *Derbyshire Papist Returns of 1705-6*, DRSS (1983)

Cliffe, J.T., *Yorkshire Gentry from the Reformation to the Civil Wars* (1969)

Clifford, J., *The Eyam Plague 1665-6* (1995)

Coates, B., 'Markets and Fairs in Medieval Derbyshire', *DAJ* vol. 85 (1965)

Cooper, B., *Transformation of a Valley, the Derbyshire Derwent* (1982)

Cox, J.C., 'Derbyshire in 1327-8, a Lay Subsidy Roll', *DANHJ* vol. 30 (1908)

Cox, J.C., *Three Centuries of Derbyshire Annals* (1890)

Cox, J.C., *The Churches of Derbyshire* (1877)

Crabtree, P.W., *Notes on Bradwell, Part II Lead Smelting*, Cave Science vol.5 (1965)

Crossley, D. and Kiernan, D., 'Lead Smelting Mills in Derbyshire', *DAJ* vol. 112 (1992)

Crutchley Papers: Court Roll of Hathersage 1547, John Rylands Library

Daniel, C., *The Story of the Eyam Plague* (1985)

Derbyshire Censuses 1841-1891

Dias, J.R., *Lead, Society and Politics in Derbyshire before the Civil War* (1981)

Directories for Derbyshire, Bagshaw (1846), White (1856), Winters (1857), Kelly (1881), Bulmer (1995)

Edwards D.G., *Derbyshire Hearth Tax Assessments 1662-70*, DRSS vol. 7 (1982)

Eyam Plague Register of St Lawrence Parish Church 1665-66 (facsimile)

Fairbank Collection, Sheffield Archives, Hathersage Enclosure Maps and Papers

Fanshaw, H.C., 'Court Rolls of Holmesfield 1481-2', *DANHJ* vols. 20-21 (1898-9)

Farey, J., *A general View of Agriculture and Minerals in Derbyshire* vol.1 (1811)

Fitzmaurice, R.M., *British Banks* (1975)

Fletcher, A., *Tudor Rebellions* (1968)

Fletcher, N., *Hathersage Parish Council, the First Hundred Years 1894-1994* (1999)

Ford, T.D. and Rieuwerts, J.H. (eds.), *Lead Mining in the Peak District* (1983)

Foster, J., *Alumni Oxonienses 1506-1856*, vol. 2-3 (1887)

Gage, J., *Collected Correspondence of J.M.W. Turner* (1980)

Garrett, H.J. (ed.), *Feet of Fines 1323-1546*, DRSS vol. 11 (1985)

Gatty, A. (ed. J. Hunter), *Hallamshire* (1869)

General City Cemetery Records, Sheffield Archives

Gloger, J. and Chester, P., *A Brief History of Needlemaking* (1999)

Glover, S., *History and Gazetteer of the County of Derbyshire, vol. 3* (1833)

Gray's Inn, Register of Admissions 1521-1889 (1895)

Grayson, P., *Derbyshire Archaeology* (1977)

Hallam, V., *Silent Valley* (1989)

Hart, C.R., 'North Derbyshire Archaeological Survey to 1500', *DAS* (1984)

Hart W.H. (ed.), *Feet of Fines, Derbyshire 1225-1323*, *DANHJ* vol. 7 (1885)

Hathersage Land Tax Records to 1832, DRO

Hathersage Parish Church Registers from 1627; Constable and Churchwarden Accounts

Hathersage Parish Council, Minutes 1894-1909, 1924-94, DRO

Hathersage Vestry Books 1821-1894, DRO

Herald's Visitation of Derbyshire made by Richard St George 1611, Harleian SS 1093

Hey, D., *Packmen, Carriers and Packhorse Roads* (1980)

Hodges, R., *Wall to Wall History, the Story of Roystone Grange* (1991)

Hodges, R. and Smith, K., (eds), *Recent Developments in Archaeology of the Peak District* (1991)

Holles, G., *Memorials of the Holles Family (1658)*, Camden Society vol. 55

Holworthy, J., Commonplace Book, transcript in Brooksbank Collection, Sheffield Archives

Hopkinson, G., 'Road Development in South Yorkshire and North Derbyshire', *THAS* vol. 10 (1976-7)

Hurst, J., *Deserted Villages* (1968)

Jackson Collection, Sheffield Archives

Jeayes, I.H. (ed.), *Derbyshire Charters* (1905)

Johnson, M.P., 'History of Grinders' Asthma in Sheffield', *THAS* (1981)

Jones, G.D.B. and Wild, J.P., 'Excavations at Brough on Noe, Navio', *DAJ* 88 (1968)

Journal of Gas Lighting, Water Supply and Sanitation Improvement, January–March 1907

Kerry, C., 'Baslow Court Rolls', *DAJ* vols. 22-3 (1900-1)

Kirby, J.W., 'A Northern Knightly Family in the Waning Middle Ages', *NH* vol. 31 (1995)

Kirke, H., 'A Derbyshire Brawl', *DAJ* vol. 24 (1902)

Kirke, H., 'Monastic Settlement in the Peak', DAJ vol. 47 (1925)

Kirkham, N., *Early Lead Mining in Derbyshire* (1968)

Lawrance, R.H. and Routh, T.E., 'Medieval Military Effigies of Derbyshire', *DAJ* vol. 47 (1925)

Lincoln's Inn, *Black Book of the Honourable Society*

Lodge, E., *Illustrations of British Topography* vol.2

Longshaw Sheepdog Trials Association, Committee Minutes from 1898

Mackenzie, M.H., 'Calver Mill and its Owners', *DAJ* vol. 84 (1964)

Marsden, B.M., *Burial Mounds of Derbyshire* (1992)

Meredith, R., 'Millstone Making at Yarncliffe in the Reign of Edward IV', *DAJ* vol.101 (1981)

Meredith, R., *The Sale of the Hathersage Estates of the Fitzherberts in the 1650s* (1970)

Meredith, R., 'The Eyres of Hassop 1470-1640', *DAJ* vol. 84-5 (1965)

Meredith, R., 'Hathersage Affairs 1720-35, Some Letters from Thomas Eyre of Thorp to William Archer of Highlow', *THAS* vol. 11 (1981)

Meredith, R., *Farms and Families of Hathersage Outseats*, Parts 1 and 2 (1982-3)

Miles, P., *Hathersage Auxiliary Hospital for Wounded Soldiers, 1914-18* (1993)

Millward, R. and Robinson A., *The Peak District* (1975)

Morgan P. (ed.), *Domesday Book, Derbyshire* (1978)

Neale, J.E., *The Elizabethan House of Commons* (1963)

Neale, J.E., *Elizabeth I and her Parliaments* vol. 2 (1957)

Newton, S.C., 'The Gentry in 17th Century', *DAJ* vol.86 (1966)

Nixon, F., *Industrial Archaeology of Derbyshire* (1969)

Ozanne, A., 'The Peak Dwellers', *Medieval Archaeology* vols 6-7 (1962-3)

Page, R.I., *Reading the Past: Runes* (1994)

Parker, V., 'Calver Mill Buildings', *DAJ* vol. 84 (1964)

Phillips Collection 1815-34, Derby Local Studies Library

Pilkington, J., *A View of the Present State of Derbyshire* (1789)

Platt, C., *Medieval England* (1978)

Platt, C., *Monastic Granges in England* (1969)

Polak, J.B., 'The Production and Distribution of Peak Millstones', *DAJ* vol. 107 (1987)

Porter, W.S., *Notes from a Peakland Parish, an Account of Church and Parish of Hope* (1923)

Postan, M.M., 'Village Livestock in 13th Century', *Economic History Review* vol. 15 (1962–3)

Radley, J. and Penny, S.R., 'Turnpike Roads of the Peak District', *DAJ* vol. 92 (1972)

Raistrick, A., *Industrial Archaeology* (1972)

Reid, R.R., *The King's Council of the North* (1921)

Rhodes, E., *Peak Scenery or Excursions in Derbyshire*, vol.2 (1822)

Richmond, I.A., *Rome and Natives in North Britain* (1958)

Robinson, B., *Walls across the Valley, the Building of Howden and Derwent Dams* (1993)

Robinson, B., *Birchinlee* (1983)

Robinson, E.V., *Hathersage Parish Church* (typescript 1944)

Roffe, D., *Derbyshire Domesday Book* (1986)

Shaw, W.A., (ed.), *Knights of England from 1257*, 2nd edn. (1971)

Shimwell, D.W., 'Capital Investment in the Expansion of a Jenny Workshop Industry in Bradwell 1799-1801', *Textile History* vol. 4 (1973)

Shuttleworth Collection, DRO

Slater, A., 'The Manufacture of Needles, Hackle Pins and Umbrella Furniture in Hathersage in 19th Century', unpublished thesis (1992)

Smith, B., *A History of the Catholic Chapel at Hathersage* (1987)

Smith, B., *Padley Chapel* (1990)

Smith, H., *Guide Stoops of Derbyshire* (1996)

Somerville, R., *The Duchy of Lancaster* (1953)

Spencer Stanhope Papers, Sheffield Archives

Stapleton, T. (ed.), *The Plumpton Correspondence*, Camden Society vol. 4 (1898)

Stirling, A.M.W., *Annals of a Yorkshire Family* (1911)

Stone, B., *Derbyshire in the Civil Wars* (1992)

Strutt Collection, Sheffield Archives

Taylor, J. (ed.), 'The Plumpton Correspondence 1416-1552', *NH* vol. 10 (1975)

Thoroton, R., *Antiquities of Nottinghamshire* (1677)

Truman, C. and Darnley, A., *Hathersage St Michael's Church of England School* (1983)

Tucker, D.G., 'Millstone Making in the Peak District of Derbyshire', *IAR* vol.8 (1985)

Turner, M., 'The Development of the South Yorkshire and North Derbyshire Coalfield 1500-1715', *THAS* vol. 7 (1957)

Turnpike Papers, Maps and Books of Reference and Statutes regarding Sparrowpit, Greenhill and Grindleford to Penistone Turnpike Trusts, DPRO, Sheffield Archives, House of Lords Record Office

Venn, J. and J.A., *Alumni Cantabrigienses* (1922)

Wightman, W.E., 'The Significance of 'Waste' in Yorkshire in Domesday Book', *NH* vol. 10 (1975)

Willie, L., 'Cupola Lead Smelting in Derbyshire', *BPDHMS* vol. 4 (1969)

Wright, S.M., 'A 15th Century Family; the Plumptons and their Lawyers', *NH* vol. 25 (1989)

Wright, S.M., *Derbyshire Gentry in the 15th Century*, DRSS vol. 7 (1983)

Yeatman, I.P., *The Feudal History of Derbyshire* (1886)

Index

Page numbers in **bold** refer to illustrations only